CHRISTIANITY
FOR GCSE

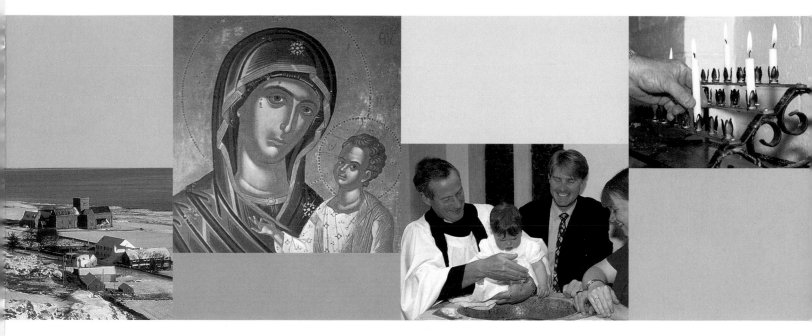

MICHAEL KEENE

John
HUNT
Publishing

Copyright © 2000 John Hunt Publishing Ltd

Text © 2000 Michael Keene

Photographs © Alex Keene

Reprinted 2003

ISBN 1 903019 57 5

Designed by
ANDREW MILNE DESIGN

Write to John Hunt Publishing Ltd
46a West Street, Alresford, Hampshire SO24 9AU, UK

The rights of Michael Keene as author and Alex Keene as photographer of this work
have been asserted in accordance with the Copyright, Designs and Patents Act 1988.

A CIP catalogue record for this book is available from the British Library.

Printed in Malaysia

Note: Throughout the series BCE [Before Common Era] and CE [Common Era]
have been used in place of the more Common BC and AD although they mean the same.

Biblical quotations taken from:
The New International Version. Hodder and Stoughton.

Picture Credits
*All photographs © Alex Keene except: p100 The Iona Community; p103 Knock Museum;
p104 Images Colour Library; p105 Hanan Isachar; p106 The Garden Tomb Association*

CONTENTS

1:1   Jesus of Nazareth

KEY QUESTION

WHO WAS JESUS OF NAZARETH AND WHAT DO WE KNOW ABOUT HIM?

Christianity, more than any other religion, is built upon the life, teaching and death of its founder, Jesus of Nazareth. The four Gospels, in the New Testament, provide us with our only real information about Jesus. The Gospels, though, are not straightforward biographies of Jesus. They were written by committed followers who used their information to make a statement about the coming of God's kingdom through Jesus, the Son of God and Saviour of humankind.

The birth of Jesus

Christianity takes its name from the Greek word 'Christ', a translation of the Hebrew title 'Messiah', meaning 'The Anointed One' – a ruler chosen and set apart by God. Whilst initially it was only a title, identifying Jesus as the Messiah, it soon became part of a proper name, Jesus Christ. The first followers of Jesus were called 'Christians', it was the obvious name to call them.

Jesus was born in the reign of Herod the Great who ruled Judea from 37 to 4 BCE as the Jewish client-king of the Romans. The mother of Jesus was Mary, a young Jewish woman, and his father was Joseph. After his birth in Bethlehem, and a short time spent in Egypt, Jesus was brought up in Nazareth, in Galilee, in northern Palestine. His upbringing was thoroughly Jewish. He was circumcised when he was eight days old, presented to God in the Temple in Jerusalem and, later, educated in the local synagogue.

BOX 1

LUKE 4.18-19

The Spirit of the Lord is on me, because he has anointed me to preach good news to the poor. He has sent me to proclaim freedom for the prisoners and recovery of sight for the blind, to release the oppressed, to proclaim the year of the Lord's favour.

[A] What is your impression of Jesus?

[B] What kind of freedom do you think Jesus came to bring - box 1?

Work to do

1 Jesus often taught about the kingdom of God. What do you think he meant by it?

2 Write a paragraph about each of the following:
a. The birth of Jesus.
b. The public life of Jesus.
c. The disciples.
d. The arrest and death of Jesus.
e. The resurrection and ascension of Jesus

The public life of Jesus

At the age of thirty Jesus left his quiet life in Nazareth to begin three years of travelling, preaching and healing throughout Judea. He taught his largely Jewish audience a new way of believing in the law of Moses and once summed this up by quoting from the Old Testament prophet, Isaiah. He told the people that hope for the captives and those who were oppressed was near to hand because God's kingdom was growing among them [box 1].

To help him in his work Jesus chose twelve close friends, his disciples, to travel with him. Much of his short public ministry was spent teaching the disciples so that they could continue his work after he left the earth. A much larger group of followers also followed Jesus, soaking up his teaching, and this group contained many women. At first, Jesus believed that he had only been sent to teach the Jews, and gather them into God's kingdom, but gradually his message was widened to include Gentiles, non-Jews, as well.

The arrest and death of Jesus

The message of Jesus soon aroused strong opposition. The Roman rulers suspected that Jesus was stirring up an uprising by the people against their control. The religious leaders believed that his actions were blasphemous because he taught the people to ignore the Jewish law. The ordinary people, though, continued to support him even whilst the religious authorities were planning his death. On the night before the plan of his enemies came together Jesus gathered his disciples together and celebrated a Passover meal with them. Christians call this meal the Last Supper.

The authorities persuaded Judas Iscariot, one of the disciples of Jesus, to betray him to them. He was arrested and taken in front of Pontius Pilate, the Roman governor of the area. Pilate wanted to release Jesus but a crowd, stirred up by their religious leaders, demanded his death. Pilate passed the death sentence which was carried out by his soldiers. A friend, Joseph of Arimathea, asked Pilate for the dead body of Jesus which was laid in his own unused tomb [box 2]. Everyone expected this to be the end of the story.

The Resurrection and Ascension

Three days after his death, when three female followers arrived to embalm the body of Jesus, they found the stone over the entrance to the tomb rolled away and the tomb itself empty. An angel told them that Jesus was alive and in the following few weeks this news was given to more and more people. They came to understand that Jesus was a new kind of Messiah – not an earthly king but the ruler of the universe. Forty days later the followers of Jesus saw him taken up into heaven. Before he left, though, he promised them that he would send his Spirit, a Comforter or Helper, to be with them. They waited until the Day of Pentecost for this to happen [1.2].

In the Glossary

Day of Pentecost ~ Disciple ~ Gospel ~ Holy Spirit ~ Last Supper ~ Messiah ~ Moses ~ New Testament ~ Old Testament ~ Passover ~ Virgin Mary

BOX 2

THE NICENE CREED, 4th CENTURY

For us men and for our salvation he came down from heaven; by the power of the Holy Spirit he became incarnate of the Virgin Mary and was made man. For our sake he was crucified under Pontius Pilate; he suffered death and was buried. On the third day he rose again in accordance with the Scriptures.

1:2 The Day of Pentecost

Luke ends his Gospel with Jesus blessing his disciples before being taken up from them into heaven. The disciples, we are told, returned happily to Jerusalem where 'they spent all their time in the Temple giving thanks to God.' *[Luke 24.52]*. Luke also opens his second book, the Acts of the Apostles, with the ascension of Jesus into heaven. As this happens, two angels appear to the disciples to tell them: 'This Jesus, who was taken from you into heaven, will come back in the same way that you saw him go into heaven'*[Acts 1.11]*.

The Day of Pentecost

The Jewish festival of Passover, during which Jesus died, was followed fifty days later by the festival of Pentecost. Jews came from all over the Roman Empire for this festival which celebrated the giving of the Torah [the Law] to Moses on Mount Sinai. Luke's description of this particular Pentecost festival was not quite history as we know it. He attempted to describe the indescribable by using highly symbolic and figurative language. Writing as an evangelist [a preacher of the Good News about Jesus] Luke was trying to persuade others to believe. We cannot be sure what happened in Jerusalem on that day but Luke's is the only description we have of the birth of the Christian Church.

For several weeks after the death of Jesus the disciples had huddled together in Jerusalem, frightened of the Romans. Jesus, though, had promised them they would receive God's power when the Holy Spirit came *[Acts 1.8]*. Jesus had also told them that they would carry his message throughout Jerusalem, Judea, Samaria and to the very ends of the earth. In Luke's description of the giving of the Holy Spirit [box 1] we are given two pieces of descriptive information:

1] The disciples heard a sound, like a rushing wind, coming from heaven.

2] The disciples saw what appeared to be flames of fire coming to rest on each one of them.

BOX 1

ACTS 2.1-4

When the day of Pentecost came, they were all together in one place. Suddenly a sound like the blowing of a violent wind came from heaven and filled the whole house where they were sitting. They saw what seemed to be tongues of fire that separated and came to rest on each of them. All of them were filled with the Holy Spirit and began to speak in other tongues as the Spirit enabled them.

[A] What did Peter say about Jesus on the Day of Pentecost?

Why do you think that Luke clothed
his description of what happened
on the Day of Pentecost in symbolic,
and miraculous, language?

Luke then went on to describe how, when they received the Holy Spirit, the disciples were able to speak in the different languages of the people in Jerusalem. Although Luke presents this as a miracle it probably meant little more than that the language of the disciples was simple enough for everyone to understand.

Peter's sermon

Throughout the ministry of Jesus Peter had been the leading disciple and the spokesman for the group. He retained this role in the early days of the Church. Within hours of the Holy Spirit being given to the disciples Peter delivered a sermon which led to 3,000 people being baptised as new believers in Jesus. In his sermon *[Acts 2.14 11]* Peter told the crowds four things about Jesus [box 2] and these beliefs formed the heart of the Christian message:

1] Jesus was God's Messiah *[Acts 2.36]*.

2] The Messiah had been crucified, buried and brought back to life again by God, the Father *[Acts 2.24]*.

3] Jesus was given the highest place in heaven as he was God's Son *[Acts 2. 32,33]*.

4] All those who repent and believe in the Gospel can have their sins forgiven by God *[Acts 2.38]*.

Today the Church that was born on the Day of Pentecost has about 1,600 million members throughout the world. Christians remember this event and the giving of the Holy Spirit when they celebrate, each year, the festival of Pentecost or Whitsun *[see 8.7]*.

> **BOX 2**
>
> **ACTS 2.38**
>
> *On the Day of Pentecost the people were greatly challenged by the preaching of Peter. He told them what to do: 'Each of you must turn away from your sins and be baptized in the name of Jesus Christ, so that your sins will be forgiven; and you will receive God's gift, the Holy Spirit.'*

[B] What was it that made the Day of Pentecost such a special, and important, day for the Christian Church?

Work to do

1 What were the key elements in the message preached by Peter on the Day of Pentecost?

2 How does Luke explain what happened to the followers of Jesus on the Day of Pentecost?

3 What do Christians celebrate at Pentecost?

In the Glossary

Ascension ~ Disciple ~ Gospel ~ Holy Spirit ~ Jerusalem ~ Messiah ~ Moses ~ Pentecost ~ Peter ~ Torah ~ Whitsun

1:3 | From One Church to Many

KEY QUESTION

HOW, AND WHY, DID THE CHRISTIAN CHURCH SPLIT UP INTO MANY DIFFERENT CHURCHES?

For many centuries after its birth there was just one Christian Church. Each individual church was led by elders or presbyters, soon to become known as priests, with groups of churches supervised by bishops. Amongst these senior priests the Bishop of Rome, the Pope, was given the greatest respect and authority. Then, in the 4th century CE the Roman Emperor, Constantine, established a second seat of power at Constantinople, in the east of his empire. A century later, in 410, the Roman Empire fell and Constantinople, rather than Rome, became the main centre of Christian spiritual activity. The two parts of the Christian world, east and west, began to drift apart. They were divided by language [Latin in the west and Greek in the east] and religious differences. A split between them was only a matter of time.

The Great Split

The split finally came in 1054 when the Eastern Churches declared themselves to be independent of those in the west. The Eastern Churches became known as 'Orthodox' ['right-thinking']. There were two main areas of disagreement:

1] The Pope in Rome claimed to have supreme power over the whole Church – east and west. The Eastern Churches did not want all of the decisions affecting them to be taken in Rome. The city was far away, and different in its thinking, to Constantinople.

2] The Eastern Churches were committed to the teachings of the Nicene Creed [see 2.1]. The Roman Catholic Church wanted to change its wording slightly and this upset the Eastern Churches.

Today, almost a millennium later, the Roman Catholic and Orthodox Churches are barely on speaking terms.

The Reformation

In the centuries that followed dissatisfaction built up within the Roman Catholic Church itself. Matters came to a head in 1517 when Martin Luther, a Catholic monk, nailed his 95 theses [grievances] against the Church to the door of his own church in Wittenburg. He attacked the Catholic Church for selling indulgences, which shortened the time someone spent in purgatory, to

[A] What divided the Eastern and Western Churches?

Talk it over

Do you think the Church would be more effective today if it was united - and one - or is the variety provided by so many different Churches important?

 In the Glossary

Baptist Church ~ Bible ~ Bishop ~ Church of England ~ Infant Baptism ~ Methodist Church ~ Monk ~ Nicene Creed ~ Nonconformist Church ~ Orthodox Church ~ Pope ~ Priest ~ Purgatory ~ Quakers ~ Roman Catholic Church ~ Salvation Army

raise money for church building. Luther maintained that the authority of the Bible was far more important than that of the Pope or the Church. His protest led to the beginning of the Reformation and the birth of the Protestant Church. The Protestant Church was born in England when King Henry VIII appointed himself to be the head of the Church instead of the Pope. Queen Elizabeth 1 later declared the Church of England to be the Established [Official] Church in the country [see 1.4]. The Protestants firmly rejected the leadership of the Pope and looked, instead, to the Bible for guidance and authority.

The Nonconformists

Before long, however, the Church of England itself began to splinter. Nonconformist Churches were born, so called because they did not 'conform' to the teachings of the Church of England. Among these Churches were:

1] The Baptist Church largely based on the teaching that adult believers, and not children, should be baptised. The Church of England insisted on infant baptism.

2] The Quakers which relied on its own brand of simple, and largely silent, worship.

3] The Methodist Church which was largely based on the teachings of a Church of England clergyman, John Wesley.

4] The Salvation Army which grew out of the teachings of Methodism to carry Christianity to the inner-city areas where the existing churches were ineffective.

Today there are over 20,000 different Churches, or denominations, in the world yet new Churches continue to be born. The modern Church is a far cry from the vision of its founder who prayed before he left the earth that all his followers might be united [see box 1].

[B] Why was the Church of England born?

BOX 1

JOHN 17.11

I pray for them. I do not pray for the world but for those you gave me, for they belong to you. All I have is yours and all you have is mine; and my glory is shown through them. And now I am coming to you; I am no longer in the world, but they are in the world. Holy Father! Keep them safe by the power of your name, the name that you gave me, so that they may be one as you and I are one.

 Work to do

1 a. Which two Churches split from each other in the 11th century?
b. What were the issues which finally brought the split about?

2 a. What was the Reformation?
b. What action triggered off the Reformation?
c. Who are the Protestants?
d. What did the Reformation achieve?

3 a. What does the word Nonconformist mean?
b. Name TWO Nonconformist Churches.

1:4 The Roman Catholic Church

KEY QUESTION

WHAT IS
DISTINCTIVE
ABOUT THE
ROMAN
CATHOLIC
CHURCH AND
ITS BELIEFS?

The Roman Catholic Church traces its history back to the apostles and, through them, to Jesus himself. This link between the distant biblical past and the Catholic Church today is maintained in two ways:

1] Through the Pope, the leader of the Catholic Church, who is believed to be the successor of Peter, the leading disciple of Jesus. Jesus himself indicated the important role given to Peter in the Church when he told him: 'You are Peter, the Rock; and on this rock I will build my church' [Matthew 16.18]. Peter was the first leader of the early Church before becoming Bishop of Rome and then suffering martyrdom in 64 CE. Successive Popes have been appointed as the Bishop of Rome and so have an unbreakable link with the apostle. They have inherited his exalted position in the Church and the authority which Jesus gave to him.
2] Through the bishops of the Church. A Church which has bishops is called 'episcopal'. As the original apostles gradually died, so bishops were appointed to take their places as leaders of the Church. The apostles passed on to the bishops their teaching authority which was intended to be passed on from one generation to the next until the end of time. This authority was transferred by the 'laying on of hands' and this tradition still finds a central place in many Catholic services such as confirmation [6.2]; ordination [4.10] and anointing the sick [5.2].

The name

The name 'Roman Catholic' is important because:
1] The 'Roman' title recognises the leadership of the Bishop of Rome, the Pope, in the worldwide Christian Church. The authority given to the office of the Pope allows him to speak, from time to time, 'ex cathedra' i.e. from the throne. When he does so his words are binding on every Roman Catholic believer.

[A] A Roman Catholic church. What does the word 'Catholic' mean?

BOX 1

MATTHEW 16.17,18

This truth did not come to you [Peter] from any human being, but it was given to you directly by my Father in heaven. And so I tell you, Peter; you are a rock, and on this rock foundation I will build my Church, and not even death will be able to overcome it.

Find out

Find out something about the background to the Second Vatican Council and why it was called. List FOUR statements by the Council which have had a considerable effect on the life of the Roman Catholic Church and the people in it.

2] The 'Catholic' title highlights the fact that the Church is worldwide and all-embracing. Catholics believe that they alone belong to the one, true Church and that all other Christians are 'separated brethren'.

Catholic worship and beliefs

The Roman Catholic Church is the largest of the Christian denominations having 60% of all believers - about 900 million people worldwide. The Church believes that its beliefs and ways of worshipping can be traced back to Jesus and his disciples. The teaching authority of the Church, known as the 'magisterium', is found in the collective ministry of all the bishops when they gather together in Church Councils. These Councils cannot change the teachings of the Catholic Church, which are fixed and eternal, but can make changes in aspects of worship. So, for instance, the Second Vatican Council [1962-5] decreed that church services could be conducted in the language of the people instead of the traditional Latin.

Amongst the most important Catholic beliefs are:

1] The Mass This service, held each day in Catholic churches, re-enacts the death of Jesus on the cross. During the Mass the bread and wine become the actual body and blood of Jesus. This is called 'transubstantiation'. A belief in transubstantiation is one of the clearest differences between Roman Catholics and Protestants.

[B] What part do bishops play in the Roman Catholic Church.

2] The Saints and the Virgin Mary All Roman Catholics are devoted to the Virgin Mary [see 2.9]. She is also a focus for devotion for Orthodox believers and Anglo-Catholic Anglicans.

3] Heaven and Purgatory All Christians believe that heaven is their destination after death but only Roman Catholics believe in purgatory - an intermediate stage between heaven and hell which prepares souls for eternal life in heaven.

Work to do

1 Write down THREE pieces of information about the office of Pope.

2 a. What is the laying on of hands?
b. Name two services in the Roman Catholic Church in which this practice is followed.
c. Why is the laying on of hands an important practice in the Roman Catholic Church?

3 What is the magisterium of the Roman Catholic Church?

4 Describe, in your own words, THREE important beliefs of the Roman Catholic Church.

In the Glossary

Anglo-Catholic ~ Anointing the Sick ~ Apostle ~ Bishop ~ Confirmation ~ Disciple ~ Episcopacy ~ Holy Spirit ~ Mass ~ Ordination ~ Orthodox Church ~ Peter ~ Pope ~ Protestant ~ Roman Catholic Church ~ Saint ~ Transubstantiation ~ Virgin Mary

BOX 2

MARK 14.22-24

While they were eating, Jesus took a piece of bread, gave a prayer of thanks, broke it, and gave to his disciples. 'Take it,' he said, 'this is my body.' Then he took a cup, gave thanks to God, and handed it to them; and they all drank from it. Jesus said, 'This is my blood which is poured out for many, my blood which seals God's covenant.'

1:5 The Orthodox Church

KEY QUESTION

WHAT IS THE ORTHODOX CHURCH AND WHICH BELIEFS HOLD IT TOGETHER?

The Orthodox Church is a federation of Churches which usually take their names from the country in which they are located. There are Russian, Serbian, Armenian and Greek Orthodox Churches amongst others and each of them is led by a senior bishop called a Patriarch. Amongst the different Patriarchs special honour is given to the Patriarch of Constantinople [the Ecumenical Patriarch] who is the spiritual leader of the Orthodox Church worldwide. There are about 150 million Orthodox believers in the world with some 400,000 worshippers in Great Britain.

The basis of the Orthodox Church

The basic belief of Orthodoxy is implied in the name itself – 'orthos' ['rightly'] and 'doxazein' ['glorify']. Orthodox believers are those Christians who see themselves as 'rightly glorifying' God since they represent the earliest form of Christianity. They follow the traditions of the faith as it was before it divided into two branches at the Great Schism [see 1.3]. The beliefs of the Orthodox Church are based on two foundations:

1] Scripture The Orthodox Church believes in the revelation of God that came through the teachings, life and death of Jesus of Nazareth. These are recorded in the Gospels. The witness of the apostles, especially Peter and Paul, contained in the New Testament complete the scriptural revelation. Down the centuries this revelation has been transmitted through the witness of the Church and continues down to the present time through the ministry of the Holy Spirit.

2] Tradition The beliefs of the Orthodox Church are summed up in the Nicene Creed [see 2.1] which is recited by everyone whenever the Holy Liturgy is celebrated. It was an attempt to change the wording of this Creed which was one of the major reasons for the split between the Roman Catholic and Orthodox Churches in 1054.

[A] This photograph shows an icon. Find out why icons are such an important feature of Orthodox churches.

▶ Work to do

1 What does the name 'Orthodox' indicate?

2 Explain the importance of the following to the Orthodox Church and the beliefs it holds:
a. The Holy Scriptures.
b. The Tradition of the Church.

3 Write TWO sentences about Orthodox beliefs on the following:
a. The Trinity.
b. Jesus.
c. The Church.
d. The Mysteries.
e. The Holy Liturgy.

The beliefs of the Orthodox Church

All Orthodox Christians believe that:

1] God is a Trinity. This means that:

a. God the Father is the creator of everything that exists.

b. God the Son was born in Bethlehem, lived amongst men and women, died on a cross and was brought back to life by his Father in heaven.

c. God the Holy Spirit was given to the world when Jesus left the earth and is now God active in the world.

2] God the Son was born as a human being to Mary. This means that the blessed Virgin Mary is the 'Theotokos', the Mother of God.

3] The Church is holy, spanning both heaven and earth. Jesus Christ, the apostles and the saints form the foundation of this Church which was originally one. All saints, both alive and dead, belong to the true Church.

4] Mysteries. All worship must centre around the sacraments – or 'Mysteries' as the Orthodox Church prefers to call

them. There are seven of these Mysteries – Holy Communion [the Holy Liturgy]; Infant Baptism [the washing away of sins]; Chrismation [Confirmation]; Marriage, Penance, Ordination to the Priesthood and Anointing the Sick. Each Mystery is a special vehicle for bringing God's grace to human beings. The most important of the Mysteries is the Holy Liturgy. It is celebrated daily in each Orthodox church as well as on special festivals and feast-days. This Mystery re-enacts the birth, life, death and resurrection of Jesus. The Holy Liturgy service provides a 'window on heaven' for Orthodox believers since its form never changes and it brings together the earthly and the eternal. This is why there is an emphasis in all Orthodox liturgy on the importance of beauty and this beauty is also an important feature of all Orthodox church buildings [see box 1].

[B] This photograph shows an iconostasis in an Orthodox church. Find out why this screen separates the altar from the people. What does it tell you about the Orthodox belief in God?

BOX 1

ARCHIMANDRE NATHANIEL

The understanding of God is the understanding of beauty. Beauty is at the heart of monastic life. The life of prayer is a constant well of beauty. We have the beauty of music in the Holy Liturgy. The great beauty of monastic life is communal life in Christ. Living together in love, living without enmity, as peaceful with each other as one dead body is peaceful with another dead body, we are dead to enmity.

1:6 | The Anglican Church

KEY QUESTION

WHAT IS THE CHURCH OF ENGLAND AND WHAT MAKES IT DIFFERENT FROM ANY OTHER CHURCH IN THIS COUNTRY?

In 597 the Catholic monk Augustine was sent by Pope Leo 1 from Rome to bring the Christian Gospel to England. When he arrived he was very surprised to discover that the Church was already well established in the country. The beliefs of the English Church, and its ways of worshipping were, however, very different from those of the Catholic Church. For some years the two forms of Christianity existed side by side but, inevitably, Catholicism prevailed. Christians in England reluctantly accepted the authority of the Pope at the Synod of Whitby in 664.

The Especial Protector

The Church in England continued to accept the authority of the Pope until 1534 when King Henry VIII declared himself to be the 'Especial Protector' of the Church [box 1]. This action by the king was prompted by the refusal of the Pope to grant him a divorce from his wife, Catherine of Aragon. Under two Acts of Parliament, in 1536 and 1539, Henry dissolved the monasteries in England, the real source of the Pope's power in this country. It was claimed that the monasteries were corrupt, and they were, but the real reason for their dissolution was that their wealth was needed to ease the king's financial problems.

By this time the birth of the Protestant religion had taken place on the continent *[see 1.3]*. Although some Catholic practices in the English Church lingered on the emphasis was now upon the Bible, and its authority, rather than that of the Pope. In 1539 a copy of the Bible, translated by Miles Coverdale, was placed in every parish church in England. Then, under Elizabeth 1, the Church of England became the 'Established Church' in England and a close link was forged between Church and State. This link remains today. All archbishops and bishops are appointed by the Prime Minister. The Archbishop of Canterbury officiates on all State occasions, such as a coronation, and bishops of the Church of England

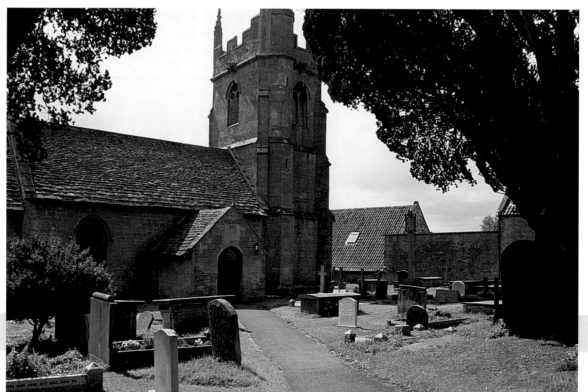

[A] The familiar face of the Church of England. Who made this Church the Established Church?

take it in turns to sit in the House of Lords. No other Church enjoys the same privileges and responsibilities as the Church of England.

The faith of the Church

A statement of faith was drawn up by the Church of England in the 16th century called the Thirty-Nine Articles. This still forms the basis of belief in the Church of England. All men and women who wish to be ordained as priests in the Church have to accept this statement of faith. The Lambeth Conference, a meeting of Anglican bishops that meets every ten years, reduced these Articles to just four basic beliefs in 1888:

BOX 1

KING HENRY VIII DECLARED HIMSELF TO BE

Especial Protector, only and supreme lord, and, as far as the law of Christ allows, even supreme head of the Church.

1] The Holy Scriptures [the Bible] contain 'all things necessary for salvation'. This was the clear teaching of the Reformation and underlines the fact that the Anglican Church is a 'Reformed' Church.

2] The Creeds [both the Apostles' and the Nicene] contain all the necessary ingredients of Anglican belief – since all of them stem from the Bible.

3] Only two sacraments, Holy Communion and baptism, need to be celebrated in an Anglican church since these are the only ones which can be traced with certainty back to Jesus.

4] The Anglican Church is an 'episcopal' Church with bishops being given the responsibility of leading the Church. Bishops were a part of life in the early Church.

 In the Glossary

Anglican Church ~ Apostles' Creed ~ Archbishop ~ Archbishop of Canterbury ~ Baptism ~ Bible ~ Bishop ~ Church of England ~ Creed ~ Episcopacy ~ Holy Communion ~ Monastery ~ Nicene Creed ~ Pope ~ Priest ~ Protestant ~ Reformation ~ Sacrament ~ Thirty-Nine Articles

[B] The Church of England now ordains women priests. Can you find out when this first happened?

Work to do

1 a. How did the Church of England come into existence?
b. What is the difference between the Church of England and the Anglican Church?

2 a. What does it mean to call the Church of England the 'Established' Church in this country?
b. List TWO ways in which the Church of England is treated differently from other Churches.
c. Can you think of ONE disadvantage to the Church of England of being the Established Church?

3 a. What are the Thirty-Nine Articles?
b. What are the four essential beliefs of the Anglican Church?

1:7 The Nonconformists

KEY QUESTION

WHO ARE THE NONCONFORMISTS AND WHAT IS DISTINCTIVE ABOUT THEM?

A number of Protestant Churches grew out of the Church of England from the 17th century onwards. These Churches were formed because their members could not 'conform' to all the teachings of the Thirty-Nine Articles. After the 1662 Act of Uniformity, which demanded a strict adherence to the Book of Common Prayer, about 2,000 clergy left the Church of England. As a result there were lasting divisions in the Protestant movement.

[A] What links the Salvation Army with the Quakers?

The Presbyterians

Presbyterianism is a form of church government in which each church is governed by 'presbyters' – elders. The Presbyterian Church, which is particularly strong in Scotland, emphasises:
1] The supreme authority of the Bible.
2] The importance of local and not central church government.
3] A simple form of worship based on readings from the Bible, hymns, prayers and a sermon.

In 1972 the Presbyterian Church in England merged with the Congregational Church to form the United Reformed Church [URC].

BOX 1

WESLEY'S CONVERSION EXPERIENCE

At exactly a quarter before nine I felt my heart strangely warmed. I felt I did trust in Christ, Christ alone, for salvation; and an assurance was given me that he had taken away my sins, even mine, and saved me from the law of sin and death.

The Quakers

The founder of the Quakers, George Fox, wanted his followers to return to the simple faith and worship of the early Christians. He called his movement 'The Society of Friends' because he wanted his followers to be friends with Jesus and each other. They were nicknamed Quakers by a judge who, at Fox's trial in 1650, was told to 'tremble [quake] at the voice of the Lord.' Quaker worship has always been based on silence interrupted only by those who have 'heard' the 'Inner Voice' of God speaking to them. They share what they have 'heard' with others. There are no ministers in the Quakers, neither do they celebrate any of the sacraments.

The Baptist Church

In 1612 the first Baptist church was opened in London based firmly on the principle that only adult believers, and not babies, should be baptised *[see 6.3]*. The only source of authority recognised by Baptists from the beginning was the Bible and they rejected infant baptism as being firmly unscriptural. Baptists also criticised the link

In the Glossary

Baptist Church ~ Bible ~ Book of Common Prayer ~ Church of England ~ Infant Baptism ~ Methodist Church ~ Protestant ~ Quakers ~ Sacrament ~ Salvation Army ~ Thirty-Nine Articles ~ United Reformed Church

Find out

The merger of the Presbyterian Church with the Congregational Church in 1972 is the only example of two Churches uniting in this country since the Second World War. Find out as much as you can about the United Reformed Church which was formed as a result.

between the Church of England and the State arguing that the Church must be free to appoint its own leaders and decide its own ways of worshipping. Instead, Baptists believe in the 'priesthood of all believers' – a belief that all church members should be free to participate in all aspects of church life [see box 2].

The Methodist Church

The Methodist Church was based on the preaching of an Anglican clergyman, John Wesley [1703-1791]. Wesley had a 'heart-warming' spiritual experience [see box 1] and this convinced him that God had taken away his sins. He travelled over 100,000 miles on horseback telling the people that God could forgive their sins as well. Charles Wesley, John's brother, wrote some of the most well-known hymns in the English language. Many of his hymns are still used in church worship today.

The Salvation Army

During the 19th century Britain had many social problems as the Industrial Revolution changed the face of the country - including illegitimacy, poverty and alcoholism. The Salvation Army, formed by the Methodist minister William Booth in 1878, established itself in the industrial inner-city areas. The organisation was run from the

beginning on military lines with a distinctive uniform and the widespread use of brass bands [A]. Most of its work was conducted in the open-air although the people contacted were invited to worship in the local citadel [a place of refuge]. Today the Salvation Army is a worldwide organisation working in 107 different countries. Like the Quakers the Salvation Army does not celebrate any sacraments.

[B] A Methodist service. What contribution did Charles Wesley make to the Methodist Church?

Work to do

1 Who are the Nonconformists and how did they come about?

2 Describe how:
a. The Baptist Movement,
b. The Methodist Church,
c. The Quakers,
d. The Salvation Army began.

3 Write down THREE pieces of information about THREE Nonconformist Churches.

4 Read box 2 carefully. There are several aspects of Baptist belief mentioned in this quote. Make a list of them in your book.

BOX 2

BAPTIST UNION STATEMENT OF BELIEF

That our Lord and Saviour Jesus Christ, God manifest in the flesh, is the sole and absolute authority in all matters pertaining to faith and practice, as revealed in the Scriptures, and that each church has liberty, under the guidance of the Holy Spirit, to interpret and administer his laws.

1:8 The Ecumenical Movement

During the 19th century Christian missionary activity throughout the world was strong but, as the century ended, many Churches began to question the competition between them to win new converts. They felt that their witness would be much more effective if they could work together. This was the beginning of the ecumenical movement. 'Ecumenism' means 'whole world' and the hope of the movement was that, one day, all of the many Churches would be united into one Church – just as it was in the beginning.

The World Council of Churches

In 1910 an assembly of 1200 delegates from 160 Protestant missionary societies, called the World Missionary Conference, gathered at Edinburgh. The delegates agreed that they should stop competing against each other. Further ecumenical initiatives followed leading, soon afterwards, to the formation of the Life and Work Movement. Then, in 1927, the Faith and Order Movement was born and this began to consider questions of actual Church unity. These two movements came together in 1948 to form the World Council of Churches [WCC]. For its first Congress 351 delegates from 147 denominations, representing 44 countries, gathered together in Amsterdam.

BOX 1

GONVILLE FRENCH-BEYTAGH. DEAN OF JOHANNESBURG

Religion means binding together.

[A] These Christians, from many different churches, have just marched together on Good Friday. Now they are erecting their crosses on a hill overlooking their city. Do you think that it is good that churches can work together in this way?

To begin with, the WCC was a Protestant movement but, significantly, the Orthodox Church joined in 1961. The Roman Catholic Church, however, remained outside, troubled by three issues:

1] The position of the Pope. Was the Pope the leader of all the world's Christians, as Catholics believe, or not? Protestants and Orthodox believers were never likely to accept his leadership.

2] The validity of the priesthood in all non-Catholic Churches. Were the priests in Protestant and Orthodox Churches really ordained? The Catholic Church did not believe that they were. Could they give the sacraments? The Catholic Church did not believe they could.

3] The real meaning of the Eucharist. The Catholic

Talk it over

Why do you think that Christians from different denominations often find it easier to work together than to tackle their differences of belief?

Work to do

1 'Christians should forget their differences and work together to help the needy.' Do you agree? Explain your response.

2 How did the Ecumenical Movement begin?

3 Describe the aims of the World Council of Churches.

4 a. Make a list of the advantages/disadvantages that there might be in having so many different Churches.
b. Do you think the Church would make a greater impact in our society if it was united?

Church believed in transubstantiation but the other Churches did not.

In 1961 the first 'Confession of Faith' was drawn up [see box 2]. In the same year the Roman Catholic Church sent observers to WCC assemblies but it has never joined the organisation. This means that in the year 2000, with over 300 Churches belonging, the WCC still does not represent more than 50% of the world's Christians.

In the Glossary

Eucharist ~ Orthodox Church ~ Pope ~ Priests ~ Protestant ~ Roman Catholic Church ~ Transubstantiation ~ United Reformed Church ~ World Council of Churches

Aims of the WCC

The World Council of Churches has two aims:
1] To develop links between the different Churches and so begin a gradual move towards unity. It was thought that if different denominations worked, and worshipped, together the other differences would not seem to be so important [see A]. From the beginning actual Church unity was thought to be only a distant possibility, if not an impossible dream, but there have been two small successes:

a. In 1972 the Congregational and Presbyterian Churches in England united to form the United Reformed Church.

b. In 1990 the Orthodox and Oriental Orthodox Churches announced that they would unite, having been separated since the 5th century.

The World Council of Churches, though, was not involved in either of these moves. Most people believe that any hope for the future lies in co-operation between churches at a local level rather than in grand schemes for unity.

2] To work together to promote justice and understanding in the world. Much of the work that the WCC has done in this area has been controversial. It has concerned itself with:

a. Helping groups fighting racism.

b. Supporting countries torn apart by war and poverty. There is a strong link between poverty and the arms race in which many poor countries are compelled to compete.

c. The growing problem of world refugees.

d. The spiritual and moral problems raised by advances in science and technology.

BOX 2

BASIS FOR MEMBERSHIP OF WORLD COUNCIL OF CHURCHES

The World Council of Churches is a fellowship of churches which confess the Lord Jesus Christ as God the Saviour according to the Scriptures and therefore seek to fulfil together their common calling to the glory of the one God, Father, Son and Holy Spirit.

1:9 The Evangelicals

KEY QUESTION

WHO ARE THE EVANGELICALS IN THE CHRISTIAN CHURCH AND WHAT DO THEY BELIEVE?

BOX I

2 TIMOTHY 3.15,16

You know who your teachers were, and you remember that ever since you were a child, you have known the Holy Scriptures, which are able to give you the wisdom that leads to salvation through faith in Christ Jesus. All Scripture is inspired by God and is useful for teaching the truth, rebuking error, correcting faults, and giving instruction for right living, so that the person who serves God may be fully qualified and equipped to do every kind of good deed.

Within the Anglican Church there are three main approaches to the Christian faith:

APPROACH ONE - THE ANGLO-CATHOLIC WAY
This places a Catholic emphasis on many beliefs and ways of worshipping. Anglo-Catholic churches emphasise the importance of the seven sacraments. In the years following the Second World War this group was dominant in the Anglican Church but its size and influence have since declined.

APPROACH TWO - THE LIBERAL WAY
This group believes that the Christian faith must change with the times. Some parts of the Bible are timeless but other parts are outdated. This group was in the ascendancy in the late 1960s and 1970s but now is losing its grip on the Anglican Church.

APPROACH THREE - THE EVANGELICAL WAY
This way teaches that the Christian faith does not change and that the Church today must live by the same principles in the Bible which have guided Christians throughout the centuries. 'Fundamentalism' is an extreme form of Evangelicalism believing that every word in the Bible was dictated by the Holy Spirit and so must be accepted as true. In the 1980s and the 1990s the Evangelicals grew in strength and influence in the Anglican Church.

There are Evangelicals in all Protestant denominations although many of them prefer to form their own independent Churches. It is thought that over 50% of Protestants are now Evangelicals. In some countries, though, the figure is as high as 80%. All of them feel strongly that they are called to deliver the gospel message of salvation in Christ through their words and actions.

Evangelical beliefs

The worldwide evangelical movement of the twentieth century has been strongly marked by an emphasis on a study of the Bible, on missionary outreach and on the basic doctrines [beliefs] of the

[A] This Evangelical church places its own creed where everyone can see it. Why do you think this is thought to be important?

Christian faith. Evangelical belief begins and ends with the Bible. The Bible is believed to be the inspired Word of God and the only revelation that God has given to us. All that we can know, and need to know, about God is found in the Bible. When a person reads the Bible today God speaks to them through it. Evangelicals usually set time aside each day to read the Bible on their own and pray. Special study-groups are held regularly in Evangelical churches to help people to understand the Bible, and its message, more clearly. In many

WHAT WE BELIEVE

About God:
God is the Creator of all things. He is powerful, loving and pure, and He is one God in three Persons- Father, Son and Holy Spirit.

About Jesus Christ:
He is Gods Son, and is both fully human and fully divine. He died on the cross in the place of sinners, He rose again from the dead, He is alive today, and He will one day personally return to earth as the Judge of every person.

About the Holy Spirit:
He is fully divine and makes the work of Jesus Christ real in the lives of believers.

About Ourselves:
Every person is a sinner by nature and therefore separated from God and under his judgment, God invites every person to turn from their sin and trust in Jesus Christ as Saviour. All who believe in Him are saved, but those who do not turn to Him in repentance and faith remain under Gods judgement.

About the Bible:
The Bible is Gods living Word and is therefore totally true. Through it He speaks to the world today, It contains all that we need to know about God, and about how we can be made right with Him and live to please Him.

churches special Bible-study sessions are held during Lent as preparation for the coming of the Easter festival. In Evangelical services a great emphasis is placed on readings from the Bible and on the sermon, based on a passage from the Bible. The Bible itself encourages believers to discover for themselves what it has to say [see box 1].

In particular, the Bible speaks about:

1] Human nature Every human being is born with a sinful nature [called 'Original Sin'] and it is this which places them under God's judgment.

Talk it over

The Evangelical approach to the Christian faith is very simple and straightforward. Do you think this is the reason why it has become very popular towards the end of the twentieth century?

In the Glossary

Anglican Church ~ Anglo-Catholic ~ Bible ~ Easter Day ~ Evangelical ~ Fundamentalism ~ Holy Spirit ~ Lent ~ Original Sin ~ Protestant ~ Roman Catholic Church ~ Sacrament ~ Second Coming

2] Salvation God in his mercy, sent Jesus, the perfect man, to be the Saviour of the world. Christ died 'in our place' by taking the sins of the world on himself. By rising from the dead Jesus conquered the power of sin for all time. Those who respond to God's message are not condemned to eternal punishment but are forgiven.

3] The Second Coming The same Jesus who died to save us from our sins will return to the earth at some future time to be its judge. Evangelicals refer to this event as 'the Second Coming'.

4] Evangelism Evangelicals believe that being 'converted' to Christ is only the beginning. Each believer is then expected to share the 'good news' about Christ with others and this is called 'evangelism'. Evangelism is a very important part of Evangelical church life.

Work to do

1 Write TWO sentences about each of the following:
a. Anglo-Catholics.
b. Liberals.
c. Evangelicals.

2 a. Describe what Evangelicals believe about the Bible.
b. Why do you think that their belief about the Bible is at the heart of their faith?

3 What beliefs, derived from the Bible, are at the heart of the Christian Gospel as Evangelicals understand it?

1:10 | Liberation Theology

KEY QUESTION

WHAT IS LIBERATION THEOLOGY AND WHY HAS IT BEEN SO CONTROVERSIAL?

Liberation Theology began in the countries of Latin America in the 1960s. It arose out of the needs of the people. The Conference of Latin American bishops in Medillin in Columbia insisted that the poor should be the main concern of the Church. This call inspired many Christians, especially Catholic priests, to take up the fight against oppression - often with violent consequences. A number of Church leaders began to teach a 'liberation theology' which encouraged the poor to act for themselves to challenge the oppression from which they suffered. Sometimes violence might need to be used before a real peace, based on justice for all, could be achieved.

Liberation Theology

At the heart of Liberation Theology stands the belief that God is on the side of all those who are poor and needy. Liberation theologians reminded everyone that:

1] In the Old Testament God heard the cry of those Jews who were in slavery in Egypt and delivered them. This is why the Old Testament prophets were passionate in calling for social justice condemning those who benefited from the misfortune of others.

BOX 1

FATHER CAMILO TORRES, COLUMBIAN FREEDOM FIGHTER

The basic thing in Catholicism is loving one's neighbour. For this love to be true it has to be effective...We must take power from the privileged minorities in order to give it to the poor majority. The revolution can be peaceful but only if the minorities who hold power do not offer violent resistance.

(A_z) **In the Glossary**

Bible ~ Bishop ~ Old Testament ~ Priest ~ Prophet ~ Protestant ~ Roman Catholic Church

---

2] In the New Testament Mary, the mother of Jesus, declared that 'God has filled the hungry with good things but the rich he has sent empty away' *[Luke 1.53]*. Throughout his ministry Jesus showed a particular concern for the hungry and poor around him. The first duty of the Church is always to support the poor.

The Bible is a very practical book. It is concerned with both the liberation of the body and the freedom of the soul. To really help the poor in oppressive countries it must concern itself with:

a. Reflection on the needs of the poor.
b. Action [praxis] to help the poor.
c. Awareness. Raising the awareness of those living in prosperity about the needs of the poor.

This teaching led many priests in Latin American countries to oppose repressive governments and some of them paid for this opposition with their lives. Sometimes, in the 1960s, the Pope criticised these priests for being too political but he also condemned those responsible for persecuting, torturing and killing them.

Base Communities

The most important practical expression of Liberation Theology has been the growth, and influence, of 'base communities.' These are small communities of fifteen to twenty poor families led by a lay-person since there is a severe shortage of priests in Latin American countries. The leaders are

Talk it over

Many people were deeply shocked by the idea of priests joining freedom fighters and being involved in violent actions. Do you think there is a place for the use of violence in trying to achieve social justice - even from Christians?

poorly educated people, often living in shanty towns themselves. The groups meet together weekly for worship, Bible-study, discussion and a growth in social awareness. The communities inform people about their situation and rights.

Sometimes they challenge governments which use murder, torture and death to keep themselves in power.

Base communities grew rapidly throughout the 1980s. There were thought to be over 100,000 such Catholic communities, involving between one and two million people, in Brazil alone. There were also Protestant base communities. In Guatemala there were 200 Protestant base communities by the middle of the decade.

> **BOX 2**
>
> **LEONARDO BOFF BRAZILIAN LIBERATION THEOLOGIAN**
>
> *Without justice and right the kingdom of God will not be established on earth.*

An assessment

Liberation Theology has aroused both support and hostility. Many in the Roman Catholic Church, including Pope Paul 11, have criticised the deep political involvement of priests in the movement. They argue that Christians should confine themselves to spiritual matters and leave politics to the politicians. Archbishop Desmond Tutu, Archbishop of Cape Town under apartheid, argued that this was a misunderstanding of Christianity. He commented: 'I am puzzled about which Bible people are reading when they suggest religion and politics don't mix.' Liberation Theology recognises that the Church must be concerned with the whole of a person's life because the God of the Bible shows the same concern.

[A] What inspiration do you think those fighting for justice receive from the death of Jesus?

 Work to do

1 a. What is Liberation Theology?
  b. Why did Liberation Theology grow?
  c. What did Liberation Theology hope to achieve?

2 What did the liberation theologians try to remind everyone about?

3 What were base communities and how were they organised?

> **BOX 3**
>
> **ARCHBISHOP HELDER CAMARA**
>
> *When I give food to the poor they say that I am a saint. When I ask why they are poor they say that I am a Communist.*

2:1 | The Creeds

KEY QUESTION

WHAT ARE THE CREEDS AND WHAT IS IN THEM?

A Creed is a statement of Christian belief. Several of them have been drawn up in the last two thousand years but only two of these – the Apostles' and the Nicene Creeds – have been widely used in Christian worship. The Roman Catholic, Anglican and Orthodox Churches still use them today in some services.

[A] The young Jesus with his mother, Mary. Beliefs about Jesus dominate the Creeds. Make a list of the different things they say about him.

The Creeds

There are tiny remnants of the earliest Christian Creeds in the New Testament. These remnants were part of a longer statement of faith taught to young Christian converts, often as part of their preparation for baptism. Short phrases have survived in the letters of Paul. The earliest of these is 'Jesus is Lord' [1Corinthians 12.3] but there are also beliefs about God the Father and the Holy Spirit found elsewhere [1Corinthians 8.6; 1Timothy 2.5-6] which probably come from early Creeds.

By the 4th century some people in the Church were teaching beliefs that others were unhappy about. Creeds were drawn up to distinguish between orthodox ['right-thinking'] and unorthodox Christians. The two most important Creeds were:

1] The Apostles' Creed Although its name suggests that it goes back to the original apostles this Creed actually dates from the late 4th century.

It may, however, have been based on the much earlier Old Roman Creed. The Apostles' Creed is shorter than the Nicene Creed and is the one used most frequently in acts of Christian worship [see box 1].

2] The Nicene Creed It was thought that this originated from the Council of Nicea, a council of bishops called by Emperor Constantine in 325 CE, but this seems unlikely. All that we know is that this Creed was being used regularly in the Eucharist service by the 5th century. The Orthodox Church still uses it today in its infant baptism service. You will find the Nicene Creed in 5.7.

What's in the Creeds?

Whilst the Creeds are of little interest to Nonconformists they still play an important role in the worship of other Churches. During most Anglican and Catholic services the people turn to face the altar and repeat the Creed, usually the

BOX 1

THE APOSTLES' CREED

I believe in God, the Father almighty, creator of heaven and earth. I believe in Jesus Christ, his only Son, our Lord. He was conceived by the power of the Holy Spirit and born of the Virgin Mary. He suffered under Pontius Pilate, was crucified, died and was buried. He descended to the dead. On the third day he rose again. He ascended into heaven and is seated on the right hand of the Father. He will come again to judge the living and the dead. I believe in the Holy Spirit; the holy, catholic Church; the communion of saints, the forgiveness of sins, the resurrection of the body and the life everlasting. Amen.

Talk it over

Do you think it surprising that Christians have not attempted to up-date the great Creeds? What could be stopping them?

Work to do

1 a. What is a Creed?
b. What do we know about the Apostles' Creed?
c. What do we know about the Nicene Creed?

2 Describe what is said in the Apostles' Creed about:
a. The Trinity.   b. Jesus.
c. The Church.   d. Life after death.

3 'The communion of the saints, the forgiveness of sins, the resurrection of the body and life everlasting.' What do you think Christians mean when they say these words from the Apostles' Creed?

4 Explain the importance to Christians today of THREE statements from the Apostles' Creed.

Apostles', together. The Creed is a unifying factor for Christians showing that, whatever might divide them, they still give their agreement to the great Christian beliefs. The most important beliefs expressed in the Creeds are that:

1] God the Father is the creator of the heavens and the earth – and everything that is in them. Although it is not expressly mentioned the Christian belief in the Trinity [see 2.2] lies behind both Creeds, particularly the Nicene.

2] Jesus Christ, God's Son, came down from heaven to be born on earth to the Virgin Mary. He became fully human; was crucified when Pontius Pilate was governor of Judea and rose from the dead on the third day. He ascended back into heaven forty days later. At some future time he will come back to judge both those still living and every one else who will be brought back to life. He will set up God's endless kingdom on earth.

3] The Holy Spirit is the third member of the Trinity along with God the Father and God the Son. He spoke through the prophets of old and is the voice of God in the world today.

4] The Church is one, holy, catholic [universal] and apostolic. The Church, in all its forms, was established by God through the apostles of Jesus and their teaching continues through its bishops, priests and members today.

5] The Church offers to the world one baptism through which all who believe can find God's forgiveness for their sins.

6] At the end of time all who have died will be brought back to life and given God's gift of eternal life.

In the Glossary

Anglican Church ~ Apostles' Creed ~ Baptism ~ Bishop ~ Creed ~ Holy Spirit ~ New Testament ~ Nicene Creed ~ Nonconformist Church ~ Orthodox Church ~ Paul ~ Priest ~ Prophet ~ Roman Catholic Church ~ Trinity ~ Virgin Mary

[B] The death of Jesus is at the heart of the Creeds. Why do you think it was believed to be so important by the early Christians?

2:2 | The Trinity

The Christian faith is built on the foundation that there is only one God. This is a belief which Christianity shares with the faith out of which it grew, Judaism. Christianity, however, goes beyond Judaism when it insists that God reveals himself to the world in three different forms – as God the Father, God the Son and God the Holy Spirit. The relationship between these three members of the Godhead is what Christians mean when they speak of the Trinity. This does not mean that Christians believe in three Gods – tritheism.

God, the Father

Three important 'truths' about God are found in the Bible. They are:

1] God is the creator of everything that exists. The Bible begins with the story of God creating the universe, the heavens and the earth. On earth God creates everything that has life including animals, birds, plants and human beings. The Bible teaches that God not only started the creative process but also continues it – God is active as the creator today.

2] God expresses his continuing interest in the world he has made just as a father and mother express their loving concern for their children –

even when they leave home. Jesus expressed this continuing interest by speaking of God caring for every sparrow and for the hairs on every human head [*Matthew 12.29-31*].

3] God is personal rather than abstract. Jesus spoke of a God with a deep personal involvement in his own life and in that of others. This is expressed in God's concern for the sufferings of Jesus on the cross.

God, the Son

Everyone is God's son or daughter since they have been created in his image. Jesus, though, is uniquely God's Son. The Incarnation, which is at the heart of Christianity, is the mystery of God being born in human flesh [*see 2.3*]. Christians believe that the same Jesus who lived and died in Palestine will return to the earth at some future time, in an event known as the 'Second Coming', to be its judge and to set up God's kingdom. Paul provided a summary of the life of Jesus which explains what early Christians believed about him in one of his letters. You can find this in box 1.

God, the Holy Spirit

Before he left the earth Jesus promised his disciples that he would send them a 'Comforter' who would constantly be with them. Christians believe that

---

[A] Why do you think that the Bible only speaks of the Holy Spirit in symbolic terms?

BOX 1

PHILIPPIANS 2.5-8

He [Jesus] always had the nature of God, but he did not think that by force he should try to remain equal with God. Instead of this, of his own free will he gave up all that he had, and took the nature of a servant. He became like a human being and appeared in human likeness. He was humble and walked the path of obedience all the way to death - his death on the cross.

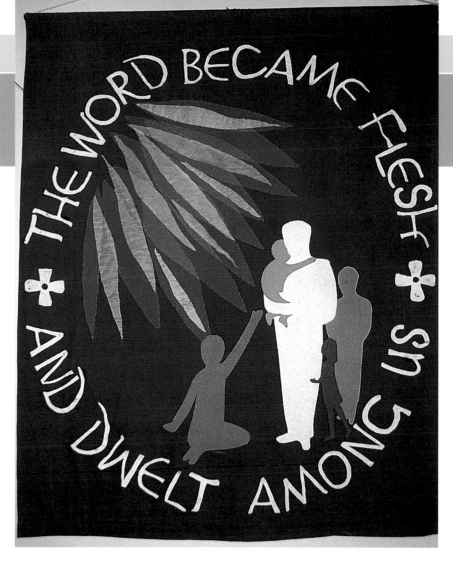

THE WORD BECAME FLESH AND DWELT AMONG US

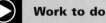

Talk it over

Christianity, like all the major world religions, believes firmly in one God. Why do you think that this is considered to be such an important belief?

Work to do

1 Read the quotation from Paul in box 1 carefully.
a. How would you explain these words of Paul: 'He was in the form of God; yet he laid no claim to equality with God'?
b. What do you think Paul meant when he said that Jesus humbled himself and took on the form of a servant?

2 a. Name the three members of the Trinity.
b. What do Christians mean when they say that they believe in God as a Trinity?

3 Explain what Christians mean when they speak of God as their Father.

4 Write down THREE things that Christians believe about:
a. God the Father.
b. Jesus, the Son of God.

this happened on the Day of Pentecost [see 1.2] when the Holy Spirit was sent by God and the Church was born. The Church would soon go through a time of great persecution and it was promised that the Holy Spirit would be an 'Advocate' who would help them to defend their faith when Christians appeared before emperors and tribunals.

To sum up

The revelation of the Trinity was expressed in the baptismal faith and worship of the early Church. It was part of the Church's worship, preaching and teaching. The Nicene and the Apostles' Creeds

[B] What do Christians mean when they refer to the 'Incarnation' ?

tried to express it in the language of the time without actually using the word itself. They were careful, in particular, to avoid giving any impression that Christians believed in three Gods. There are not three Gods – only God in three Persons. The Trinity is a matter of revelation:

1] God the Father has shown himself to the world as the creator who sent Jesus to the world to save it.

2] Jesus showed the world what God was like. Without the picture of God provided by Jesus we would know very little.

3] God continues to make himself known today through the Holy Spirit.

BOX 2

PROFESSION OF FAITH OF POPE PAUL VI

We believe in one God, Son and Holy Spirit, creator of all things visible - such as this world in which our brief life runs its course - and of things invisible - such as the pure spirits which are also called angels.

In the Glossary

Apostles Creed ~ Bible ~ Disciple ~ Holy Spirit ~ Incarnation ~ Nicene Creed ~ Trinity ~ Virgin Birth ~ Virgin Mary

2:3 | The Incarnation

KEY QUESTION

WHY IS IT
IMPORTANT FOR
CHRISTIANS TO
BELIEVE THAT
JESUS WAS BOTH
FULLY DIVINE
AND FULLY
HUMAN?

The Incarnation [the birth of God as a human being] is the greatest mystery of the Christian religion. Christians believe that God became man in Jesus to take away the sins of the world – and to show the love of God to everyone. The mystery began when an angel announced the birth of Jesus to Joseph with the words: 'You shall call his name Jesus, for he will save his people from their sins' *[Matthew 1.21]*. Clearly this was intended to be no ordinary birth or life.

God and Man

The Christian Church has always believed two fundamental things about Jesus of Nazareth around which everything else in the Gospels revolves:

1] Jesus was the Son of God – and so divine. Occasionally, in the human life of Jesus, his divine nature can be glimpsed in the Gospels. One such occasion was the baptism of Jesus when a voice, the voice of God, spoke to him out of heaven *[Luke 3.21,22]*. Another was the Transfiguration *[Luke 9.28-36]* which looked forward to the glory which was going to be revealed after Jesus rose from the dead.

2] Jesus was the Son of Man – and so human. The Incarnation is all about the birth of God on earth. Mary was the human mother of Jesus although Jesus was not conceived in her womb by Joseph.

The father of Jesus was the Holy Spirit. This belief is called the Virgin Birth and is not accepted by all Christians. It maintains that Mary was still a virgin when Jesus was born. Roman Catholics believe that she remained a virgin for the whole of her life *[see unit 2.9]* but other Christians do not accept this. Orthodox Christians call Mary 'the Mother of God' [Theotokos].

The humanity of Jesus

The story of Jesus told in the four Gospels emphasises that he was, in every possible way, a human being. He displayed the whole range of natural human emotions and needs – anger, hunger, thirst, disappointment, despair and love. The unknown writer of one of the letters in the New Testament spoke of Jesus in this way: 'For it is not

BOX 1

LUKE 1.32,33

He will be great and will be called the Son of the Most High God. The Lord God will make him a king, as his ancestor David was…his kingdom will never end.

[A] What belief about Jesus is expressed in this traditional crib scene?

UNTO US A SON IS GIVEN

[B] Why do Christians believe that God sent his Son into the world?

Work to do

1 Write a ONE sentence definition explaining what Christians mean when they talk about the 'Incarnation'.

2 Why do Christians believe that God became a man in the person of Jesus?

3 Explain what Christians mean when they apply these two titles to Jesus:
a. The Son of God.
b. The Son of Man.

4 How do the Gospels present a picture of the human side of Jesus?

as if we had a high priest who was incapable of feeling our weaknesses with us; but we have one [Jesus] who was tempted in every way that we are; though he is without sin' [Hebrews 4.15].

These two sides of the character of Jesus can be seen in the two titles which are given to him in the Gospels more frequently than any others:
1] The Son of God - emphasising the divine side of his nature and his relationship with God.
2] The Son of Man - emphasising his human side and his affinity with other human beings. Interestingly no-one else used this title of Jesus in the Gospels. Jesus, though, often referred to himself as the Son of Man. It was as if others were afraid to suggest that God himself was sharing their lives with them on earth.

Christians believe that both sides of the character of Jesus are equally important, as the Apostles' Creed makes clear. Without being God Jesus could not have died so that the sins of the world would be forgiven. He could not have shown the love of God in his life, words and death unless he had a unique relationship with his Father. At the same time he was fully human. It was only by being this that Jesus was able to share fully in the joys and sufferings of other human beings. Paul had in mind both the divine and the human qualities of Jesus when he commented that 'the mystery of our religion is very deep indeed.'

BOX 2

MARK 1.11

As soon as Jesus came up out of the water, he saw heaven opening and the Spirit coming down on him like a dove. And a voice came from heaven, 'You are my own dear Son. I am pleased with you.'

BOX 3

JOSEPHUS, FIRST CENTURY JEWISH HISTORIAN

It was at that time that a man appeared - if 'man' is the right word - who had all the attributes of a man but seemed to be something greater. His actions, certainly, were superhuman for he worked such wonderful and amazing miracles that I cannot for one regard him as a man; yet in view of his likeness to ourselves I cannot regard him as an angel either.

In the Glossary

Apostles' Creed ~ Baptism ~ Gospel ~ Holy Spirit ~ Incarnation ~ New Testament ~ Orthodox Church ~ Paul ~ Roman Catholic Church ~ Virgin Birth ~ Virgin Mary

2:4 | The Atonement

KEY QUESTION

HOW DOES THE TEACHING OF THE NEW TESTAMENT HELP US TO UNDERSTAND THE MEANING OF THE DEATH AND RESURRECTION OF JESUS?

The death and resurrection of Jesus stand at the very centre of the Christian faith. You become aware of this whenever you enter a church, especially a Roman Catholic one. There you will find the fourteen Stations of the Cross [a series of pictures or sculptures] which trace the last few hours in the life of Jesus. They follow through from the condemnation of Jesus by Pontius Pilate to the moment when his body was laid in Joseph of Arimathea's unused tomb. Crucifixes and crosses on the altar and elsewhere emphasise the Christian belief that the death and resurrection of Jesus go to the very heart of the faith. Christians particularly remember these events on Good Friday and Easter Sunday *[see units 8.5 and 8.6].*

BOX 2

1 CORINTHIANS 15.17-19

If Christ has not been raised, your faith is futile; you are still in your sins. Then those also who have fallen asleep [died] in Christ are lost. If only for this life we have hope in Christ, we are to be pitied more than all men.

The Death of Jesus

The four Gospels give us different accounts of the sequence of events that led up to the death of Jesus on the cross. They all go on to describe how Jesus, the Son of God, rose from the dead. The remainder of the New Testament, especially the epistles [letters] of Paul, attempt to present the meaning and importance of these two events. It does so by giving us a series of 'pictures' which we can piece together, rather like a jigsaw, to understand how the Church understands the immense significance of the death and resurrection of Jesus.

1] Jesus defeated the powers of evil by his death. The last few hours of the life of Jesus, spent on the cross, saw a conflict going on between the powers of good and evil. This conflict can be seen throughout the life of

Jesus from the time that he was tempted in the wilderness by Satan *[Luke 4.1-13].* The resurrection of Jesus from the dead is the final proof that the powers of God's goodness triumphed over darkness in the end.

2] Jesus brought together [reconciled] God and human beings by his death. In the opening chapters of the Bible the first man and woman sinned against God. They were thrown out of paradise [the Garden of Eden] and a great barrier sprung up between God and the human race – the barrier of sin. Jesus, the sinless Son of God, brought the two sides together by his death. Sinful human beings are brought into a state of friendship with God through the death of Jesus. In the New

BOX 1

ROMANS 5.8,9

God has shown us how much he loves us - it was while we were yet sinners that Christ died for us! By his blood we are now put right with God; how much more, then, will we be saved by him from God's anger.

[A] Where would you be likely to find a cross or a crucifix in a church?

[B] What do Christians believe is demonstrated by the resurrection of Jesus?

In the Glossary

Atonement ~ Bible ~ Crucifix ~ Easter Day ~ Epistle ~ Good Friday ~ Gospel ~ Jerusalem ~ Mass ~ New Testament ~ Old Testament ~ Roman Catholic Church ~ Satan ~ Stations of the Cross

Testament this is called the 'atonement'.

3] Jesus, the supreme example. Jesus was the supreme example to us all of self-giving love. He accepted all the pain and suffering which his life involved. Towards the end Jesus did not find it easy to accept God's will. He fought strongly against it in the Garden of Gethsemane *[Mark 14.32-42].* Finally, though, he gave in and accepted the will of God - even though this resulted in his death. In accepting the pain which is a part of being really human Jesus left us all an example to follow.

4] Jesus was a sacrifice. To deal with sin in the Old Testament a perfect animal was sacrificed and its blood spread over the altar of the Temple in Jerusalem. Through his death Jesus offered himself to God as the perfect sacrifice. He became the lamb of God who takes away the sins of the world

Find out

Every Roman Catholic church has fourteen Stations of the Cross around its walls. Find out what the different stations represent and how they play an important part in the church's worship on Good Friday.

for ever. We have been disobedient to God but, through his obedience, Jesus allows us to share in his own sacrifice. Roman Catholics believe that this is what happens each time they celebrate Mass.

The resurrection of Jesus

Christians believe that the resurrection of Jesus completes all that Jesus did on the cross. Paul expresses his opinion that the death of Jesus would have been a waste if God had not brought him back to life [see box 2]. The event sets God's seal on all that Jesus taught and did. If the powers of darkness could not keep the body of Jesus in the tomb then they cannot have ultimate power over human beings either. The resurrection of Jesus shows that the power of Satan has been finally broken.

Work to do

1 What different 'pictures' are used in the New Testament to explain the importance and meaning of the death of Jesus?

2 Why do you think that the cross is the most important Christian symbol?

3 What does the word 'atonement' mean and what is the link between it and the death of Jesus?

4 a. Why might a Christian celebrate the death and resurrection of Jesus Christ?
b. Suggest ways in which this celebration might help the Christian in his or her daily life.

2:5 | The Holy Spirit

After Jesus left the world the disciples were huddled together for some time in Jerusalem. Jesus had told them to remain in the city until God sent them the power that they needed to carry out his work. Luke, the author of the Acts of the Apostles, described what happened when the Holy Spirit was given to the disciples: 'When the day of Pentecost came, they were all together in one place. Suddenly a sound like the blowing of a violent wind came from heaven and filled the house where they were sitting. They saw what seemed to be tongues of fire that separated and came to rest on each one of them. All of them were filled with the Holy Spirit…' [Acts 2.1-4].

BOX 1

ROMANS 5.5

The love of God has been poured into our hearts by the Holy Spirit which has been given to us.

The language that Luke used is, of course, highly symbolic. In his description he used two symbols to describe the coming of the Holy Spirit. They were:

1] WIND Everyone in Jerusalem was amazed at the power of the Spirit's coming. Yet it was not 'power' in the normal sense of the word that overwhelmed them. The power in question was that of God's love and it was this love that they were to share so successfully with the world. Paul wrote about this kind of power in the quotation in box 1.

2] FIRE In the Bible fire is a symbol for the purifying work of God in the human heart. It was as purifying 'tongues of fire' that God took over

[A] Why do you think that the Day of Pentecost is often called 'the birthday of the Christian Church'?

the disciples on the Day of Pentecost. Fire in the Bible symbolises cleansing. After they were cleansed by God's Spirit the disciples went out to preach fearlessly throughout the Roman Empire. Many of them were to be put to death in the years to come for their faith. The most notable of the martyrs were Peter and Paul who both died in the persecution instigated by the Roman Emperor, Nero, in 64 CE.

Apart from the work of the Holy Spirit in bringing God's power and cleansing to those who believe, the Bible also provides us with another important symbol for the Spirit of God. This

What do the symbols of fire, wind and a dove suggest to you? How do you think these symbols can help people to understand the work of the Holy Spirit today?

Acts of the Apostles ~ Bible ~ Communion of Saints ~ Creed ~ Day of Pentecost ~ Disciple ~ Holy Spirit ~ Jerusalem ~ Liturgy ~ New Testament ~ Passover ~ Paul ~ Priest ~ Trinity

symbol has its origins in the book of Genesis where, in the story of the flood, Noah released a dove and it brought back an olive-leaf in its beak to show that the waters had receded *[Genesis 8.8-1]*. In the New Testament, when Jesus was baptised, the Holy Spirit descended from heaven on him in the form of a dove *[Matthew 3.16]*. The dove symbolises the peace of God which is brought to the world through his Spirit [B].

The work of the Holy Spirit

The Church is the place where the Holy Spirit can be experienced. The Church believes that the Holy Spirit:

1] Inspired the writing of the Scriptures and still speaks to people through them. This is why the Bible plays such an important part in public and private worship. People who read and listen to the Scriptures are hoping to hear the voice of God.

2] Works through the words of the liturgy [set patterns of worship] to inspire people in their worship of God. Most of the liturgies used in Christian worship are very old and tested ways of expressing the praise and prayers of the people. This is especially true of the Orthodox Church where the liturgy goes back to the 4th-century CE.

3] Helps all believers as they struggle to pray [see box 2]. Paul says that the Spirit prays for us when we struggle, and often fail, to find the appropriate words for ourselves.

4] Is in the work of the Church, its priests and all lay-people as they struggle to build up the kingdom of Christ on earth.

When Christians stand during a service, face the altar and say in the words of the Creed, 'I believe in

> **BOX 2**
>
> **ROMANS 8.26**
>
> *The Spirit too comes to help us in our weakness. For when we cannot choose words in order to pray properly, the Spirit himself expresses our plea in a way that could never be put into words.*

the Holy Spirit,' they are simply asking for God's help. They receive that help through reading the Bible, praying and drawing on the help and support of the Church. They also draw inspiration from the lives and witness of those who have lived before them and are now part of the Communion of Saints.

[B] What does the symbol of the dove for the Holy Spirit indicate?

▶ **Work to do**

1 Explain the meaning, and the symbolic importance, of the following symbols used in the New Testament for the Holy Spirit:
a. A dove.
b. Fire.
c. Wind.

2 Explain what it is that Christians believe about the Holy Spirit.

3 How did the first Christians receive the Holy Spirit?

2:6 | Pictures of the Church

KEY QUESTION

HOW IS THE CHURCH DESCRIBED IN THE NEW TESTAMENT AND WHAT PICTURES ARE THERE TO HELP US UNDERSTAND IT?

The word 'church' can be used in three different ways: a] The Church is made up of all Christians throughout the world. b] The Church is a local group of Christians who meet for worship in a particular church building. c] The church is any group of Christians, large or small, who meet together to worship and pray.

The Church is one, holy, catholic and apostolic

The Nicene Creed contains the words: 'We believe in one, holy, catholic and apostolic Church.' What does this description mean?

1] The Church is one This means that the worldwide Church is united. There may be many different Churches but underlying these divisions the Church is one. The reason is that each Christian, of whatever denomination, is united with Christ and Christ is united with all who belong to the Church [A].

2] The Church is holy God is holy and the Church is one with God. Being holy means 'being separated from sin' and this is what the Church should be.

3] The Church is catholic The word 'catholic' here means 'universal or worldwide'. In this sense we are not referring to the Roman Catholic Church but to the Church which is found throughout the world. Whatever denominational label the Church in a particular place may carry it is part of the worldwide Church.

4] The Church is apostolic The Church was born on the Day of Pentecost in the time of the apostles. The authority of the apostles was passed down to bishops. Bishops today have the same role as the apostles of old – to preach, teach and administer the sacraments. Both the Roman Catholic and the Orthodox Churches claim to have direct descent from the apostles of Jesus.

Two helpful pictures

There are two pictures of the Church which figure prominently in the New Testament. These give us a helpful insight into the way that the early Christians saw the Church:

1] *Picture 1* The Church as the people of God. Throughout the Old Testament the Jews are the Chosen People of God looking for their Messiah, the leader sent by God. Most of the early Christians were Jews and they believed that Jesus was the long-expected Messiah. They also believed that the Christian Church was the new people of God. All people who belonged to the Church were united around baptism, a common faith and the sacraments. The Church is a family into which all who believe in Jesus have been born. They are 'sons', 'daughters', 'brothers' and 'sisters' in Christ. They are united together by the love of God spread abroad in

---

BOX 1

EPHESIANS 4.2-6

Be completely humble and gentle; be patient, bearing with one another in love. Make every effort to keep the unity of the Spirit through the bond of peace. There is one body and one Spirit - just as you were called to one hope when you were called - one Lord, one faith, one baptism; one God and Father of all, who is over all and through all and in all.

BOX 2

THE SECOND VATICAN COUNCIL

The head of the body is Christ. He is the image of the invisible God and in him all things came into being…He is the head of the body which is the Church. He is the beginning, the firstborn from the dead, that in all things he might hold the primacy. All members must be formed in his likeness, until Christ be formed in them.

1 The Nicene Creed says: 'We believe in one, holy, catholic and apostolic Church.' Explain the meaning and significance of each of these FOUR descriptions of the Church.

2 Choose TWO pictures of the Church found in the New Testament. Explain how they help us to understand the role of the Church.

3 Paul spoke of the Church as being 'the BODY of Christ'. What did he mean when he used this picture?

their hearts by the Holy Spirit.

2] *Picture 2* The Church as the body of Christ. Paul speaks of the Church fellowship as the 'body of Christ' [see box 1]. The Church, he said, is like a human body with Christ as the head. Just as there are many parts to the human body so there are many parts to the Church. Just as every part of the human body must play its role so every part of the Church body must play a part as well. As Paul stressed, the welfare of the Church as a whole is much more important than the health of its individual members.

In particular, the head and the body are close. The head provides a sense of direction and is the basis of the body's health and strength. In a similar way the health of the body [the Church] depends totally on the strength it draws from its head [Christ]. Within the Church there are many sources of unity:

a. Its allegiance to God through Jesus Christ. The one God is 'Father of all, who is over all, and through all and in all.'

b. The Holy Spirit's inspiration.

c. The faith which all Christians share with each other.

d. The one baptism which opens the door to church membership.

[A] How do you think someone might argue that the Church was united even if there were many different Churches?

Apostle ~ Baptism ~ Holy Spirit ~ Messiah ~ New Testament ~ Nicene Creed ~ Old Testament ~ Orthodox Church ~ Paul ~ Pentecost ~ Roman Catholic Church ~ Sacrament

2:7 | Authority in the Church

KEY QUESTION

HOW IS
AUTHORITY
EXERCISED IN
THE DIFFERENT
CHRISTIAN
CHURCHES?

There are rules and guidelines for people who want to belong to any of the Christian Churches. There are also, within each Church, individuals or groups of people who have been given authority and responsibility. Across the different Churches it is expected that this authority should be used in the same spirit of love which always characterised the life of Jesus [see box 1].

Sources of authority

There are marked differences between the different Churches over where they believe that God's authority is to be found. Here are three examples:

1] The Baptist Church Most Christian Churches accept that the Bible is, in some sense, the Word of God although they differ over just what this means. The Bible is the only source of authority in the Baptist Church. Each Baptist church is independent although many of them do belong to the Baptist Union. The Union, however, is only responsible for organising those aspects of church life which cannot be arranged locally – the training of Baptist ministers, the organisation of missionary work overseas, etc.

Each Baptist church elects a group of men and women to take its own decisions. These men and women are called 'deacons' and the group together is known as a 'diaconate'. The minister in a Baptist church is often called the 'pastor' [shepherd] and he is appointed by the diaconate. Decisions within the church are taken and the worship is organised as far as possible along biblical lines. No other source of authority is recognised. Much care is taken,

BOX 1

MARK 12.30,31

Love the Lord your God with all your heart and with all your soul and with all your mind and with all your strength...Love your neighbour as yourself.

[A] St Peter. Explain why this disciple of Jesus has particular significance for the Roman Catholic Church.

Some Churches exercise a greater control over their members in the areas of belief and morals than others. To what extent do you think individual Christians should be left free to make up their own minds on these issues?

1 Explain where authority is believed to lie in a Baptist church.

2 a. What does it mean to call the Church of England a 'Protestant' Church?

b. The Lambeth Conference laid down four pillars on which the authority of the Anglican Church was said to stand. What are they?

c. On the question of authority what similarities and differences does the Anglican have with the Baptist Church and the Roman Catholic Church?

3 The Roman Catholic Church recognises three sources of authority. Write TWO sentences about each of them.

therefore, to educate church members about the teachings of the Bible since they are expected to live by its principles.

2] The Anglican Church The Anglican Church, as the Baptist Church, is Protestant. They were both formed after the Protestant Reformation, in the 16th century, which broke the hold of the Roman Catholic Church in Britain and other continental countries. The key belief of the Reformation was the sufficiency of the Bible to determine all matters of church and personal belief. The Church of England is part of the worldwide Anglican Church. The Anglican Church bases its authority on the Bible, the two Creeds, the two sacraments of the Eucharist and infant baptism and the orders of bishops, priests and deacons.

BOX 2

JOHN 13.34-35

A new command I give you: Love one another. As I have loved you so you must love one another. By this all men will know that you are my disciples, if you love one another.

3] The Roman Catholic Church The Roman Catholic Church recognises three sources for its beliefs:

a. The Bible.

b. Church Tradition and Councils. The Pope can call a General Council of the Church, to which all bishops belong, at any time but, in practice, this rarely happens. In fact there have only been three of them since the 16th century - the Council of Trent [1545-1563]; the First Vatican Council [1869-70] and the Second Vatican Council [1962-5]. The Roman Catholic Church believes that its bishops carry the same authority which Jesus gave to his disciples. Anything which meets the unanimous approval of the bishops becomes part of the tradition of the Church.

c. The Pope. The Pope, the head of the Roman Catholic Church, is believed to be St Peter's successor on earth [box 3]. The Pope has the authority to speak infallibly and when he does this he is said to be speaking 'ex cathedra' [from the throne]. Anything he then says becomes part of the faith of the Church. In practice, though, this only happens occasionally. He is much more likely instead to give guidance on matters of belief or morals by issuing an 'encyclical'. Sometimes the encyclical causes disquiet amongst Catholic believers. This happened in 1968 when Pope Paul VI issued the encyclical Humanae Vitae which ruled out the use of artificial contraceptives for all Roman Catholics.

In the Glossary

Anglican Church ~ Apostles' Creed ~ Baptism ~ Baptist Church ~ Bible ~ Bishop ~ Church of England ~ Creed ~ Disciple ~ Episcopacy ~ Eucharist ~ Minister ~ Nicene Creed ~ Peter ~ Pope ~ Priest ~ Reformation ~ Roman Catholic Church

BOX 3

MATTHEW 16.18-19

And I tell you that you are Peter, and on this rock I will build my church, and the gates of Hades [hell] will not overcome it. I will give you the keys of the kingdom of heaven and whatever you loose on earth will be loosed in heaven.

2:8 | Suffering

KEY QUESTION

WHAT PROBLEMS DOES SUFFERING IN THE WORLD CAUSE THE CHRISTIAN WHO BELIEVES IN A LOVING GOD?

Suffering is a universal experience which affects everyone, to a greater or lesser extent, at some point in their lives. To Christians, who believe in a loving God, this suffering presents a great challenge to their faith. This challenge comes not just from the 'fact' of suffering but also from the unfairness of it all. Some people suffer much more than others. Natural disasters cause widespread devastation in some parts of the world but not in others. In some countries countless adults and children die from malnutrition whilst in others people have more than enough to eat. The problem which all this causes can be simply stated:

Either God wants to relieve suffering but cannot, in which case he is not all powerful, **or** God can remove suffering but chooses not to do so, in which case he is not all loving.

Explaining suffering

There are four suggested 'answers' to suffering in the Bible:

1] Suffering is caused by sin. This was the basic view held by people in the time of Jesus and it lay behind the encounter between Jesus and the blind man [John 9]. People even believed that children could suffer for the sins of their ancestors - up to four generations! Passing the man his disciples asked Jesus, 'Teacher, whose sin caused him to be born blind? Was it his own or his parents' sin?' Jesus rejected the idea that the man's sickness was the result of any sinful behaviour - but then curiously remarked that the man's blindness was brought about so that 'God's power might be seen to be at work in him.' If you think about it that answer causes even more problems!

2] God alone knows the reason for a person's suffering and awkward questions should not be asked - suffering must be accepted. Life and death are both in the hands of God. The classic book on suffering is that of Job in the Old Testament and this is the conclusion he reached [box 1]. Yet how can anyone see suffering on an immense scale - whether caused by earthquakes, cyclones or flooding - and not ask questions?

3] Suffering comes from the misuse of human freedom. To some extent this is true. A man smokes forty cigarettes a day for thirty-five years and dies of lung cancer as a direct result. It may seem a harsh judgment but only one person can be blamed for the outcome. It is a simple case of cause and effect. Yet much illness is not the result of misusing the body. Accidents happen which are no fault of the person who suffers. Babies are born with congenital deformities through no fault of their own.

BOX 1

JOB 1.21

Naked I came from the womb, naked I shall return whence I came. The Lord giveth and the Lord taketh away; blessed be the name of the Lord.

▶ Work to do

1 Which forms of suffering cause you most concern? Explain why.

2 Some people maintain strongly that the presence of widespread suffering in the world makes it impossible for people to believe in a loving God. Do you agree with them? Explain your answer.

3 Explain ONE way in which a Christian might seek to help a person who is suffering.

4 How might a Christian cope with his or her own suffering?

5 'Suffering can be of benefit to people.'
a. Describe THREE examples of suffering which could be of benefit.
b. Do you think that these examples might justify some forms of suffering?

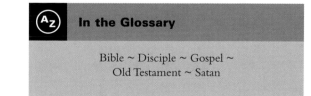

CHRIST DIED FOR OUR SINS

🔄 **Talk it over**

Imagine a world in which most, if not all, forms of suffering had been removed. Do you think that this kind of world would be 'heaven on earth' or would it present its own very special kinds of problems?

Christianity and suffering

There are two main ways in which Christianity deals with the problem of suffering. It emphasises:

1] The suffering which Jesus, the Son of God, underwent on the cross [A]. Without this suffering he could not have died for the sins of the world. When Jesus suffered and died it was God himself suffering and dying [box 2]. Yet Jesus overcame death and rose to new, and eternal, life. Suffering is a challenge to all to find a new, inner strength and to live in the light of the resurrection of Jesus from the dead.

2] After death, the suffering of this life will be forgotten in the joy of eternal life. This is the reason why the vast majority of Christians continue to believe in a loving God, even though there are many experiences in this life which would seem to suggest otherwise. They have their eyes firmly fixed on the eternal life which lies beyond death.

BOX 2

DIETRICH BONHOEFFER, MARTYRED GERMAN CHURCH LEADER

God is weak and powerless in the world, and that is precisely the way, the only way, in which he is with us and helps us…Only the suffering God can help.

🔤 **In the Glossary**

Bible ~ Disciple ~ Gospel ~ Old Testament ~ Satan

[A] How might a Christian find that the death of Jesus helps them to cope with their own suffering?

4] Suffering is brought about by the activity of Satan, the Devil. In the Gospels Satan is the evil power, a fallen angel, who opposes God. He was the one who tempted Jesus in the wilderness *[Matthew 4.1-11]*. Some Christians today still explain suffering by blaming the Devil.

2:9 | The Virgin Mary

KEY QUESTION

WHAT BELIEFS ABOUT THE VIRGIN MARY AND HER PLACE IN WORSHIP ARE HELD BY THE DIFFERENT CHRISTIAN CHURCHES?

All of the main Christian Churches believe that Mary was the mother of Jesus. The Churches do not agree, however, on the role that the Virgin Mary should play in belief and worship. There are three different approaches to this:

1] The Virgin Mary is given an important place of honour and respect in the life and worship of the Roman Catholic Church. Chosen by God to give birth to Jesus, the Son of God, her role as 'Mother of God and the Redeemer' means that she '…far surpasses all creatures, both in heaven and earth' [Second Vatican Council]. There are statues of the Virgin Mary in every Roman Catholic church [A and B]. Sometimes candles are lit in front of the statue and the help of Mary is sought as a person prays.

2] The Orthodox Church gives honour and respect to Mary as they do to all saints. She is the object of religious devotion as well and this is stimulated by her painting appearing on many icons.

3] Protestants do not believe that Mary was different from any other human being. She was chosen by God to give birth to Jesus – but no more. She is not given any place of honour in the worship of Protestant Churches and her help is not sought in prayers offered to God.

Who was Mary?

Mary is only referred to by name in the Synoptic Gospels and the Acts of the Apostles - nowhere else in the New Testament. Two Gospels, Matthew and Luke, carry a description of the birth of Jesus before which, according to Luke, Mary received a visit from an angel. The angel informed her that she was to give birth to Jesus, God's Son. When Jesus started to preach Mary accompanied him on some of his early journeys. She was present when he turned water into wine at a wedding-feast in Cana in Galilee [John 2.1-11]. She was on the end

[A] In which churches would you be most likely to see a statue like this?

BOX 1

A ROMAN CATHOLIC PRAYER

Alone of all women, Mother and Virgin, Mother most happy, Virgin most pure, now we sinful as we are, we honour thee as how we may with our humble offerings; may the Son grant us that by imitating thy most holy manners, we also, by the grace of the Holy Ghost, may deserve spiritually to conceive the Lord Jesus Christ in our inmost soul, and once conceived never to lose him. Amen.

Find out

Protestants do not share the same devotion to Mary as is found in the Catholic and Orthodox Churches. Find out why this is.

 Work to do

1 Explain what Roman Catholics mean by:
a. The Virgin Birth.
b. The Immaculate Conception of the Virgin Mary.
c. The Assumption of the Virgin Mary.

2 Describe what the Roman Catholic Church teaches about the Virgin Mary.

of some very sharp words from him on this occasion – as she was later when she attempted, with his brothers, to stop him preaching *[Matthew 12.46-50]*. She was also present at the cross when Jesus was crucified *[Matthew 27.56]*. Jesus told John, one of his disciples, to look after Mary after he died.

Mary and the Catholic Church

The Roman Catholic Church holds three specific beliefs about Mary:

1] She was a virgin when Jesus was conceived and she remained a virgin for the whole of her life. The Nicene Creed makes it clear that the early Church believed that Jesus was 'born of a virgin'. This simply means that he was conceived in the womb of a virgin without sexual intercourse taking place. Joseph was not his natural father. Matthew *[1.18-25]* and Luke *[1.26-38]* explain this by saying that he was conceived supernaturally by God the Holy Spirit. Strangely, though, the remainder of the New Testament says nothing about the Virgin Birth.

2] She was immaculately conceived. From the 15th century the Roman Catholic Church believed that Mary was free from original sin the moment she was conceived in her mother's womb. This made her different from every other human being since they have all been born with a natural tendency to sin. Mary, though, was sinless. This belief became part of the official teaching of the Roman Catholic Church in 1854.

3] She was taken straight up to heaven, body and soul, at the end of her life without dying – just as Jesus was. Mary now reigns at the right hand of her Son as Queen of heaven. This belief, called the 'Assumption of the Virgin Mary', is one which Catholic and Orthodox believers alike share. Both Churches celebrate the Feast of the Assumption on August 15th. Although Orthodox Christians have held this belief for centuries it only became an official Roman Catholic doctrine in 1950.

[B] Why would you be unlikely to see a statue like this in a Protestant church?

 In the Glossary

Acts of the Apostles ~ Gospel ~ Icon ~ New Testament ~ Nicene Creed ~ Original Sin ~ Orthodox Church ~ Protestant ~ Roman Catholic Church ~ Saint ~ Synoptic Gospels ~ Virgin Birth ~ Virgin Mary

BOX 2

CATECHISM OF THE CATHOLIC CHURCH

The Church...by receiving the word of God in faith becomes herself a mother. By preaching and baptism she brings forth sons and daughters who are conceived by the Holy Spirit and are born to God, to a new and immortal life.

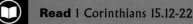 **Read** 1 Corinthians 15.12-22

2:10 | Life After Death

KEY QUESTION

WHAT DO CHRISTIANS BELIEVE ABOUT LIFE AFTER DEATH AND JUDGMENT?

Christians have always held strong beliefs about life after death. These are reflected in the different funeral services which are held across the various denominations. Underlying everything is the conviction that death is not the end and that the soul [the spiritual part of each person] survives death. Furthermore, at the end of time, the body will be resurrected to share in Christ's victory over death.

Funeral services

The Orthodox Church believes that death is God's punishment for sin and so is a human tragedy. In amongst the tragedy, however, there is hope and this is expressed in the funeral service by the lighting of candles and the spreading of incense. Everyone is encouraged in the funeral service to look forward to the return of Christ to the earth when everyone will be raised from the dead. The living and the dead will then be reunited.

Both Orthodox and Catholic believers pray for the dead. In a Catholic church these prayers begin on the night before the funeral when the body is taken to the church. Unlike Protestants, however, Catholics believe that the soul goes to purgatory – a place located between heaven and hell – after death. The amount of time spent there can be directly affected by the prayers of those who are still alive. This is why praying for the dead is an important Catholic activity.

Whilst Protestants do not believe in purgatory they do believe strongly in life after death. This is why the soul of a person who has died is committed to the safe keeping of God as their body is lowered into the grave. The prayers and Bible readings in a Protestant funeral service reflect the belief that once a person has died their soul is with God in heaven. Everyone then looks forward to the end of time when all Christian believers will receive a 'new body' similar to the one that Christ had when he returned from the dead. This will happen when Christ returns to the earth - as he promised to do.

BOX 1

ROMANS 8.38,39

Neither death, nor life, nor angels, nor principalities, nor powers, nor things present, nor things to come, nor height, nor depth, nor anything in all creation, will be able to separate us from the love of God in Christ Jesus our Lord.

▶ Work to do

1 Explain what Christians believe about judgment and life after death.

2 'You can't be a Christian without believing in life after death.' Do you agree?

3 What, in your opinion, are the main arguments for and against believing in life after death?

4 What beliefs about life after death are shown in Christian funerals?

5 Why do Roman Catholic and Orthodox believers pray for the souls of those who have died whilst Protestants do not?

Judgment

The final judgment of all people is a theme that runs through the Bible and the Creeds of the Church. Here are two examples:

1] **The Apostles' Creed** 'He shall come again to

Talk it over

Most of the reasons put forward for believing in life after death are 'religious'. Do you think that there are any 'non-religious' reasons why people might also believe in a life after death?

In the Glossary

Apostles' Creed ~ Bible ~ Creed ~ Nicene Creed ~ Orthodox Church ~ Protestant ~ Purgatory ~ Roman Catholic Church ~ Second Coming

[A] What part of a person is believed by Christians to survive death?

judge the living and the dead.'
2] **The Nicene Creed** 'He ascended to the heavens and shall come again to judge the living and the dead.'

BOX 2

THE CATECHISM OF THE CATHOLIC CHURCH

Death is the end of our earthly pilgrimage, of the time of grace and mercy God offers us so that we may work out our ultimate destiny by lives led in keeping with his plan…

The time is coming when God the Father will reveal the truth about everyone's life – the good that they have done and the evil that they have inflicted on others [John 5.28-29]. This time of judgment will coincide with the return of Christ to the earth [Matthew 25.13, 31]. This event is known by Christians as the Second Coming. Whatever sins it has committed the Church will then be presented to Christ as a pure and spotless 'bride'.

The Roman Catholic Church, however, believes that there are two forms of judgment:

a. An individual judgment in which each man and woman will be called to give an account of themselves to God. This takes place at death.
b. The general judgment of the world which is linked to the second coming of Christ.

BOX 3

THE METHODIST SERVICE BOOK

Eternal God, the Lord of life, the conqueror of death, our help in every time of trouble, comfort us who mourn, and give us grace, in the presence of death, to worship you, that we may have sure hope of eternal life and be enabled to put our whole trust in your goodness and mercy, through Jesus Christ our Lord. Amen.

3:1 The Sacred Scriptures

The Bible, the holy book for all Christians, is actually a collection of books which is divided into two parts - the Old Testament [39 books] and the New Testament [27 books]. Roman Catholics also include a further seven books from the Apocrypha in their Bible - books that were written between the ending of the Old Testament and the beginning of the New. The Orthodox Church adds another five books to the Apocrypha. Protestants, though, do not believe that the books of the Apocrypha should be ranked alongside the other books in the Scriptures.

The Old Testament

The Old Testament in the Christian Bible contains the same books as in the Jewish Scriptures - although the books are in a different order. In the Jewish Scriptures there are three divisions:

1] The books of the Law These are the first five books of the Old Testament - Genesis, Exodus, Leviticus, Deuteronomy and Numbers. In the Jewish Scriptures these form the first division - the Torah. They contain the foundation documents of the Jewish faith - the creation of the world, the Exodus from Egypt, the giving of the Ten Commandments, the entry of the Jews into their Promised Land of Canaan - and so are most highly respected by the Jewish people. The Torah also contains the 613 laws which God gave to the Israelites and which still form the basis on which most Jews live their lives today. Amongst the laws are those that govern punishment, religious worship and the animals that can and cannot be eaten. The Ten Commandments stand at the centre of these laws. Although Jesus gave his followers

BOX I

AMOS 5.11-12

You trample on the poor and force him to give you grain. Therefore, though you have built stone mansions, you will not live in them; though you have planted lush vineyards, you will not drink their wine. For I know how many are your offences and how great are your sins.

'new laws' to follow he was careful to indicate that his laws did not replace those of the Torah but completed them [Matthew 5.17-20]. He clearly had the greatest possible respect for the Ten Commandments [Luke 18.18-30].

2] The books of the Prophets A 'prophet' was a man who 'forthtold' the message of God. He may have been speaking about the future but he was much more likely to be talking about the present - and the judgment of God upon the way that the people were behaving. Amos, for example, writing in the 8th century BCE reminded the people that God was just and that he expected the people to treat each other properly. You can find an example of the strong language that Amos used in box 1. The books of the Prophets in the Jewish Scriptures

Apocrypha ~ Bible ~ Exodus ~ Gospel ~ Jerusalem ~ Messiah ~ New Testament ~ Old Testament ~ Orthodox Church ~ Prophet ~ Prophets ~ Protestant ~ Roman Catholic Church ~ Satan ~ Ten Commandments ~ Torah ~ Writings

1 a. What is the Apocrypha?
b. How many books from the Apocrypha does the Roman Catholic Church include in its Scriptures?
c. How many are included by the Orthodox Church?
d. What is the Protestant attitude to the Apocrypha?

2 a. Into which three divisions are the Jewish Scriptures divided?
b. Which of these sections is most highly valued by the Jewish community - and why?

3 Write short notes on each of the following:
a. The Torah.
b. The Prophets.
c. The Writings.

[A] What is the relationship between the Jewish Scriptures and the Old Testament?

laws. They promised that God's judgment would fall on a people who so consistently ignored these laws. Most of the prophets, major and minor, looked forward to the coming of a future leader, the Messiah, who would deliver Israel from its enemies. Christians believe that Jesus was this promised leader sent from God.

3] The Writings Most of the Writings are books of poetry and include both the Psalms and the Proverbs. Many of the Psalms were written to be used in worship in the Temple in Jerusalem. The book of Job tells the story, in poetic form, of an innocent man who loses everything, including his family, because Satan wished to test his faith in God. The Song of Solomon, traditionally thought to have been written by the Old Testament king of the same name, is a series of erotic love poems. Christians value these writings, especially the Psalms, for the things that they say about God. The singing of some of the Psalms are still included in the more traditional acts of church worship. You can find the most well-known Psalm in box 2.

fall into two groups:
a. The Major Prophets. These refer to three of the prophets - Isaiah, Jeremiah and Ezekiel - each of whom have long books written in their names. It is very unlikely, though, that any of the writing came from them.
b. The Minor Prophets. The last twelve books in the Old Testament are much shorter and are named after prophets who lived between the 8th and 4th centuries bce. Most of them were highly critical of the way that the people were living and especially of the lack of social justice in a society which claimed to be living by God's

---

BOX 2

PSALM 23.1-4

The Lord is my shepherd, I shall not be in want. He makes me to lie down in green pastures, he leads me beside quiet waters, he restores my soul. He guides me in paths of righteousness for his name's sake. Even though I walk through the valley of the shadow of death, I will fear no evil, for you are with me; your rod and staff they comfort me.

3:2 | The New Testament

KEY QUESTION

WHAT IS
THE NEW
TESTAMENT
AND WHAT DOES
IT CONTAIN?

[A] What is at the heart of the story told in the New Testament?

Christians believe that the twenty-seven books of the New Testament complete the story of God's salvation which was begun in the Old Testament. At the heart of the New Testament is the story of how God sent the promised 'Messiah', his chosen leader, to bring salvation to the world through his death and resurrection. That person was Jesus.

The New Testament

The New Testament contains many writings by the early Christian leaders and these were placed alongside the books in the Old Testament to form the Bible that we know today [see 3.3]. The books of the New Testament can be grouped into two main sections:

1] The Gospels and the Acts of the Apostles

Just as the books of the Torah are at the heart of the Jewish faith so the four Gospels provide the foundation documents on which the Christian religion is built. They tell the story of Jesus on earth through from his birth to his death on a cross and his resurrection from the dead. The books are called Gospels because they contain the 'good news' of the coming of Jesus into the world. They were written for two reasons:

a. To teach converts to Christianity the basic information about the life of Jesus. To begin with most of the converts were Jewish, with a knowledge of the Old Testament, but, before long, people from a pagan background were joining the Church. They had no knowledge at all of the Scriptures or of the stories of Jesus. They needed to be able to read about Jesus for themselves.

b. To encourage Christians to share the good

BOX 1

1 CORINTHIANS 13.4-13

Love is patient, love is kind. It does not envy, does not boast, is not proud. It is not rude, is not self-seeking, it is not easily angered, it keeps no record of wrongs. Love does not delight in evil but rejoices with the truth. It always protects, always trusts, always hopes, always perseveres. Love never fails…And now these three remain: faith, hope and love. But the greatest of these is love.

Work to do

1 What do Christians believe about the link between the Old Testament and the New Testament?

2 Write short notes on each of the following:
a. The Gospels.
b. The Epistles.

news of Jesus with others - and to provide them with a tool to help them. The Gospels are not straightforward biographies of Jesus. They are written by people who have committed themselves to Jesus and want others to share their faith.

The first of the Gospels, Mark, was not written until about 65 CE - more than thirty years after Jesus had died. During the intervening period the stories about Jesus had been passed around the Christian community, and kept alive, mainly by word of mouth. One or two of them might have been written down but if so these documents have long since been lost. Two other Gospels, Matthew's and Luke's, were written within fifteen years of Mark's. These three Gospels together give us a similar picture of Jesus and have much of their material in common. Because of this they are called 'Synoptic ['seeing together'] Gospels'. They all move through the life of Jesus, and his teaching, but concentrate on the last few days of his life - and his resurrection from the dead.

The fourth Gospel, John's, is very different from the other three. To begin with it was not written until the last few years of the first century - some sixty years after the death of Jesus. It does not share much material with the other three Gospels although they all broadly agree on the events surrounding the death of Jesus. John's Gospel is mainly made up of the teaching of Jesus - very little of which is found in the other Gospels.

The Acts of the Apostles which follows the four Gospels in the New Testament takes up the story after Jesus ascended into heaven. It describes the story of the early Church in the largely hostile Roman Empire. The dominant character in the first part of the book is Peter but he is soon replaced by Paul.

2] The Epistles or Letters The bulk of the New Testament is made up of letters written by the early Church leaders - especially Paul. There are twenty-one of these letters altogether. Paul was not one of the original disciples but was converted to Christ through a dramatic experience on the road to Damascus [*Acts 9.1-19*]. After his conversion Paul became a tireless missionary - making three long, and arduous, preaching journeys through the Roman Empire. During these travels he made many converts and established churches in which they could worship. Later, he wrote letters to some of these new churches, and his converts, explaining to them the basics of Christian belief and life. Some of the letters were long and complex - such as those written to the Christians in Rome and Corinth - but others were much briefer [see box 1]. Peter, James and John also wrote letters included in the New Testament. These letters are important to Christians today because they provide an insight into the way that the early Christian groups organised themselves - and some of the problems that they faced.

[B] This page shows the opening of the Acts of the Apostles. What is this book in the New Testament about?

 In the Glossary

Acts of the Apostles ~ Bible ~ Epistle ~ Gospel ~ Messiah ~ New Testament ~ Old Testament ~ Paul ~ Peter ~ Synoptic Gospels ~ Torah

3:3 | The Canon of Scripture

Every religion has its own collection of Holy Scriptures which members of that faith accept as authoritative. The collection itself is called the Canon from the Greek word meaning 'measuring rod'. The Scriptures provide the standard alongside which every belief and all behaviour can be judged. The Canon of the Christian Scriptures covers all sixty-six books in the Bible. They were originally included in the Scriptures because the spiritual value of each book was recognised and valued [see box 2]. There were, however, some books over which considerable doubt was expressed.

The Jewish Scriptures

Most of the books which the Jews accepted as authoritative were widely recognised as such by the time of Jesus. Whenever reference is made in the Bible to the 'Scriptures', as it frequently is in the New Testament, it is to these Jewish Scriptures that the writer is referring. Most of the early Christians were Jews and they would have been familiar with these holy books. Although the Jewish canon was not finally fixed until the Synod of Jamnia in 90 CE there was general agreement about the content of the Jewish Scriptures long before then. Since the Christians did not yet have a New Testament,

however, they did not use the term 'Old Testament' to refer to the Jewish Scriptures. This term was first used, as far as we can tell, around 170 CE.

The New Testament

The writers of the books in the New Testament frequently quoted from the Jewish Scriptures. They did this because they were anxious to demonstrate that the coming of Jesus, and what happened to him, was foretold centuries earlier by the prophets of Israel. The Gospel writers and Paul, in particular, frequently referred to the Jewish Scriptures. We do not know how many of the books in the New

[A] When was the canon of the Jewish Scriptures settled?

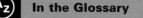

Talk it over

Why do you think that many Christians would want to insist that God was involved, in some way, in the choice of the books which were later included in the Bible?

[B] What was Peter's link with Mark's Gospel?

Testament were written by Paul but he was certainly the most prolific of its authors. He wrote his first letter, 1 Thessalonians, around 50 CE which made it the earliest book in the New Testament. In fact, all of the books of Paul were written before the first Gospel.

The books written by the apostles and other church leaders, especially Paul, were very highly valued by the young Christian Church. The apostles were people who had had first-hand experience of being with Jesus and had information about him that was not in general circulation. Although Mark, for instance, was not a disciple his Gospel was largely based on the recollections of Peter, the most important disciple of Jesus. The letters of Paul were circulated far more widely than simply to the people to whom they were first sent. All of the churches in an area read the letters of Paul to their congregations.

People and congregations began to make a collection of the different books that were being circulated. Soon these were put together into a kind of 'unofficial Bible'. Justin Martyr, who lived between 100 and 165 CE, spoke of the 'New Testament'. Certainly, by the end of the second century most of the books that are in the New Testament today were accepted as being special and God-inspired in some way – although there was disagreement over one or two of them. Hebrews, 2.Peter and Jude were viewed with suspicion for some time. In 367 Athanasius, an influential bishop of the Eastern Church, set out his own Canon which contained twenty seven books. The same Canon was confirmed at the Synod of Carthage in 397 and the selection of books in the New

In the Glossary

Apostle ~ Bible ~ Canon ~ Disciple ~ Gospel ~ New Testament ~ Old Testament ~ Paul ~ Prophet ~ Roman Catholic Church

Testament has remained the same ever since. The Roman Catholic Church accepted this although, surprisingly, it did not agree officially on the canon until the Council of Trent was held in the 16th century.

Work to do

1 a. What was the attitude of the early Christians to the Jewish Scriptures?
b. What use did they make of them?

2 How was the New Testament written?

3 a. What is meant by the word 'Canon'?
b. How was the word 'Canon' applied to the Old and New Testaments?
c. How was the canon of the New Testament settled?

4 Why did the early Christians want to include the Jewish Scriptures as part of their Bible?

BOX 1

DEFINITION. THE OXFORD DICTIONARY OF WORLD RELIGIONS

Canon: The determination of books which have authority in a religion, either because they are believed to be inspired or revealed, or because they have been so designated. In Christianity…the decision about which books were to be included or excluded was a long process.

BOX 2

OWEN CHADWICK: A HISTORY OF CHRISTIANITY

The 'canonical books' were the books which established 'the rule of faith', as distinct from other books which might be good but did not have the same authority.

3:4 | God's Word

The Bible is of great importance to Christians since it carries God's authority in all matters of belief and behaviour. Most Christians give it this authority because they believe that it had a divine origin. Paul spoke of the Scriptures as being 'God-breathed' adding that no-one could know anything about God unless he had chosen to reveal himself *[2 Timothy 3.16,17]*. It is in this sense that the Bible is 'God's Word'.

Authority

Christians believe that the final authority for their beliefs and actions come from three different sources:

1] The Church and its traditions
2] A person's conscience
3] The Bible

The attitude of Christians to the question of authority depends largely on the religious tradition from which they come. Protestants, for example, give supreme authority to the teachings of the Bible. Any authority given to the Church or individual conscience only applies when teachings from these two sources dovetail in with the teaching of the Bible. When the two conflict then the Bible is supreme. Roman Catholics, on the other hand, believe that Church tradition and the Bible together provide the guidance and help that believers need. You can see this clearly in the quotation in box 2. The Word of God was entrusted to the apostles by Christ and the Holy Spirit and this is faithfully recorded in the Bible. The teachings of the Church support, and extend, this record. Together they provide all that someone needs to follow the Christian life.

The Bible as God's Word

The phrase 'the Word of God' is deeply rooted in Christian worship. Very often the readings from the Bible which form an important part of such worship are introduced by a reference to 'God's Word'. The meaning of the phrase, though, is very difficult to pin down since it means different things to different people:

1] Fundamentalism It may mean that God spoke, his words were recorded in the Bible and so the holy book is inerrant i.e. without error. This makes the words of the Bible God's direct word to human beings. Nothing in the Bible can be untrue or misleading - it is the direct Word of God. People who believe this are called 'fundamentalists'.

2] Evangelical It may mean that the words of God were transmitted directly to human beings who

[A] Why do many Christians consider the study of the Bible to be so important?

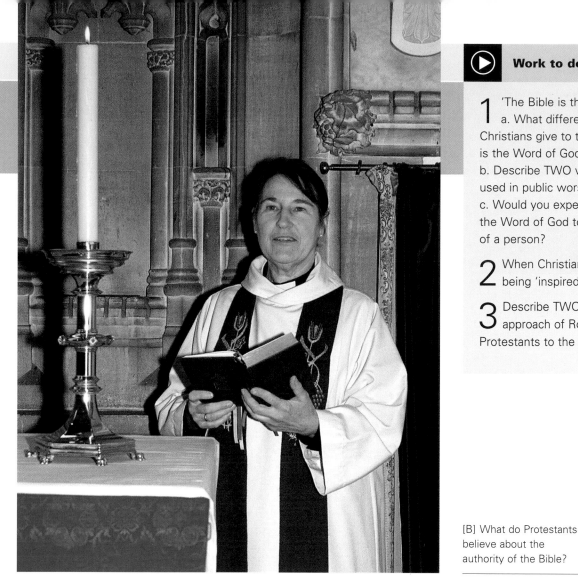

Work to do

1 'The Bible is the Word of God.'
  a. What different interpretations might Christians give to their belief that the Bible is the Word of God?
  b. Describe TWO ways in which the Bible is used in public worship.
  c. Would you expect a belief in the Bible as the Word of God to affect the everyday life of a person?

2 When Christians speak of the Bible being 'inspired' what do they mean?

3 Describe TWO differences in the approach of Roman Catholics and Protestants to the question of authority.

[B] What do Protestants believe about the authority of the Bible?

BOX 2

THE CATECHISM OF THE CATHOLIC CHURCH

Sacred Scripture is the speech of God as it is put down in writing under the breath of the Holy Spirit. And Holy Tradition transmits in its entirety the Word of God which has been entrusted to the apostles by Christ the Lord and the Holy Spirit. It transmits it to the successors of the apostles so that, enlivened by the Spirit of truth, they may faithfully preserve, expound and spread it abroad by their teaching. Both Scripture and Tradition must be accepted and honoured with equal sentiments of devotion and reverence.

recorded it – sometimes imperfectly – in their own words. This allows the reader to glimpse the individual personalities of the writers through what they have written but the authority of the Bible, God's Word, cannot be doubted. This is the Evangelical viewpoint [see 1.9].

3] Liberal Although the writers were inspired to write the books of the Bible by the Holy Spirit they were only human – and so they made mistakes. They were also influenced by the attitudes and ideas of their time. Many of those ideas are no longer accepted today. They shared, for example, the common attitudes of the time towards women and so did not allow them to play a central role in church life. Today things have moved on and the Church is perfectly justified in rejecting this aspect of the Bible's teaching. The Bible contains the Word of God but is not, in its entirety, God's Word.

In the Glossary

Bible ~ Holy Spirit ~ Minister ~ Paul ~ Priest ~ Protestant ~ Roman Catholic Church

One of the tasks of priests and ministers is to determine what is, and what is not, God's word in the Bible.

Christians, therefore, do not agree on how the Bible should be understood. Take, for example, the story of the creation of the world [Genesis 1-3]. To the fundamentalist this passage teaches that the world was made by God in six literal days of twenty-four hours each. The Evangelical understands the creation story to be a description of a historical event although it contains some symbolic elements – such as 'days' representing periods of time. For the Liberal, however, the story is full of symbolic meaning exploring the theme of God creating the world – although it contains little of scientific or historical value. To find out how the world was really made we must turn to the scientist and not to the Church.

You can find out how the Bible is used in worship, both private and public, by looking at unit 4.9.

4:1 | Cathedrals

In the Church of England and the Roman Catholic Church churches are grouped together into dioceses, a geographical area over which a bishop exercises leadership and control. In each diocese one church is set aside as the church of the bishop, the cathedral. This is not necessarily the largest, or most beautiful, church in the diocese. The bishop often leads worship in the cathedral but he does not take all the services. He is also expected to visit other churches in the diocese regularly, often to carry out special services such as confirmation. In many large dioceses there are assistant bishops ['suffragan bishops'] who have responsibility for some of the churches and also sometimes deputise for the bishop.

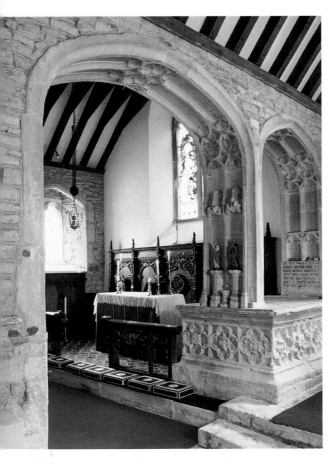

[A] How was the sanctity of cathedrals often preserved in the past - and why was this necessary?

Cathedrals

The word 'cathedra' means 'a chair or a throne'. It was used originally of the chair on which the bishop sat in the most important church in his diocese which was very close to his own residence. In the early days worship in this church was carried out by the bishop and his own household or 'familia'. The bishop conducted Mass there for his own 'family' of priests. Later, however, the responsibilities of the bishop greatly increased and a separate group of clergy became responsible for day-to-day worship in the cathedral. This group became known as the 'chapter'. The bishop only visited the cathedral for the more important services.

In the 19th century many Church of England dioceses were formed and new cathedrals were created. Often an existing church was given the status of a cathedral. In Southwark and Bradford, for example, parish churches became cathedrals. In Truro, Guildford, Coventry and Liverpool new cathedrals were built. Since 1850 in the Roman Catholic Church several new cathedrals have been established. The most important of these have been at Westminster, in London, and Liverpool. The city of Liverpool now has a Roman Catholic and an Anglican cathedral, both presided over by a bishop.

BOX 1

FROM 'A-Z OF THE CATHOLIC CHURCH'

The cathedral of a diocese is the church in which the bishop has set up permanently his episcopal seat [Latin: cathedra]. It is usually situated in the town from which the diocese is named, and which is the residence of the bishop. The date of the cathedral's consecration and its titular saint are kept as feasts in the diocese. A cathedral has a chapter of canons whose duties ordinarily include the chanting of the Divine Office.

In the Glossary

 Talk it over

Altar ~ Anglican Church ~ Bishop ~ Cathedral ~ Confirmation ~ Diocese ~ Mass ~ Requiem Mass ~ Roman Catholic Church ~ Saint

Why do you think that every community needs to come together, from time to time, to express its feelings of great happiness or sadness?

The importance of cathedrals

In the Middle Ages cathedrals became far more than simply places of worship. The nave, for instance, was often used by local traders to carry on their business. To safeguard the worship side of the cathedral's life screens were built to block off the altar so that the Mass could be celebrated without outside interference. These screens, of wood or stone, were called 'rood screens' because they usually had a large 'rod' [cross] as part of their design. The screen was usually richly carved with saints, emblems, etc, as well. Most of the rood screens have now been removed from churches and cathedrals to open up the worship to the people in the congregation.

Today, though, many people prefer to be closer to the worship than the traditional cathedral allows. They need to feel a part of the worship in which they are participating. When a new Roman Catholic cathedral was being planned for Liverpool the architects were told that everyone in the building should be able to see the altar clearly and that no-one should be further away than twenty-three metres. The result was a round building in which everyone was seated around the central altar. Today cathedrals are frequently used to bring together communities, often at times of great sadness or need. People congregate in them from all over the diocese. When the Hillsborough football disaster took place in 1989 a special Requiem Mass was held in the Roman Catholic Cathedral of Liverpool to express the grief of the whole city.

[B] What is the 'chapter' of a cathedral?

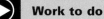 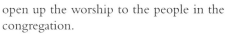 **Work to do**

1 Imagine that you are a bishop who is giving instructions to an architect for the design of a new cathedral. List FIVE points that you would particularly ask the architect to bear in mind and explain why.

2 Explain: a. What a diocese is.
b. Who a bishop is.
c. What a cathedral is.

3 a. Why are cathedrals so called?
b. How have the responsibilities of bishops changed ?
c. How might a new cathedral be different from an older one?

4:2 | A Catholic church

KEY QUESTION

WHAT ARE THE KEY PARTS OF A ROMAN CATHOLIC CHURCH AND WHAT DO THEY SYMBOLISE?

Although Roman Catholic churches were traditionally built in the shape of a cross many new ones, built during this century, are circular or semi-circular. The change is important. The new buildings, with everyone close to the altar, show that everyone is equal in the sight of God. The Second Vatican Council [1963-65] ordered that the high altar should be moved away from the east wall of a church so that the priest could stand behind it, and face the people, when he was celebrating Mass.

[A] What important objects can you see in this photograph?

A Roman Catholic church

In the typical Roman Catholic church there are several distinctive elements:

1] The Stoup Worshippers entering a Roman Catholic church will find a small container holding holy water, just inside the door [B]. As they enter the church they dip two fingers into the water and trace the 'sign of the cross' over their body. To do this the fingers move from head to breast across the shoulders from left to right [in the Orthodox Church the fingers move from right to left]. The worshipper mutters the words, 'In the name of the Father and the Son and of the Holy Spirit,' as the fingers move across the body. The water symbolises the new life, and cleansing, that everyone can find in God's Church.

2] The Font The font, just inside the door, holds the water that is used when a baby is baptised - see 6.1. Its position reminds everyone that baptism is the 'door' into the Church. For this reason infant baptism is, along with Confirmation and the Eucharist, one of the 'sacraments of initiation'. In some churches, however, the font is placed in the middle of the congregation as a reminder that

baptism brings a baby into the heart of the Christian family which takes on the responsibility of nurturing and developing its spiritual life.

3] The Altar In traditional churches the altar stands, together with a crucifix and candles, in front of the east wall of the church. This position for the altar was chosen so that when worshippers faced the altar they were also looking eastwards towards the rising sun and the holy city of Jerusalem. A tabernacle [a small cupboard] stands to one side of the altar or in a side-chapel. The Reserved Sacrament of bread and wine is kept in the tabernacle. This has already been blessed by the priest and is used every time the Mass is celebrated - whether in the church or in a person's home.

BOX 1

IAN, ROMAN CATHOLIC, AGED 18

'I went through a rebellion against the Church when I was in my early teens but I find it more meaningful than ever now. Above all else I find my local church a haven of peace and quiet, especially when my life is becoming too hectic. It helps me to worship God when I am surrounded by so many reminders of his presence.'

Talk it over

Roman Catholic churches are full of symbolism. Why do you think that symbols are such an important part of Christian worship?

In the Glossary

Altar ~ Baptism ~ Confirmation ~ Crucifix ~ Eucharist ~ Font ~ Good Friday ~ Holy Spirit ~ Jerusalem ~ Mass ~ Maundy Thursday ~ Orthodox Church ~ Priest ~ Reserved Sacrament ~ Sacrament of Reconciliation ~ Second Vatican Council ~ Stations of the Cross ~ Virgin Mary ~ Votive Candle

Originally a rood screen blocked the altar off from members of the congregation but most of these have long since been removed. The crucifix on the altar contains a figure of Christ to help worshippers meditate on the death of Jesus. From time to time during the Christian Year, as on Maundy Thursday and Good Friday, the crucifix and other pieces of furniture in church are covered up or removed altogether.

4] The Virgin Mary As we saw in 2.9, the Virgin Mary, the mother of Jesus, is very important to Roman Catholics. Catholics believe that she entered the world sinless and left it without experiencing death. Worshippers often pray in front of her statue after lighting a candle. They pray for help and guidance whenever they have an important, or difficult, decision to make. Elsewhere in a church worshippers often light a votive candle before praying. Candles, symbolising the light of God, play a very important role in Catholic worship.

5] Around the church Around the walls of a Catholic church there are fourteen pictures, or carvings, illustrating the different Stations of the Cross. These Stations show the different places where Jesus is thought to have stopped on his way

to the cross in Jerusalem. On Good Friday the worshippers process around the different Stations, stopping to think and pray at each one of them in turn [see 8.5]. In most Catholic churches there are also confession cubicles where people can confess their sins to a priest and receive the Sacrament of Reconciliation [see 5.3]. Since the Second Vatican Council, however, people have been able to confess their sins without going into a cubicle and some modern Catholic churches do not have them at all.

Find out

The second Vatican Council has been described as the most important event in the Roman Catholic Church in the 20th Century. Find out THREE things that changed in the Roman Catholic Church as a result of this Council.

Work to do

1 a. Describe a typical altar that you would find in a Roman Catholic church.
b. Describe two ways in which the altar is used.
c. Why was the altar placed against the east wall in old churches and why has this now changed?

2 A Roman Catholic church is full of symbolism. What is symbolised by:
a. The holy water in the stoop?
b. The candles?
c. The elements in the Reserved Sacrament?

[B] Why do Roman Catholics mark themselves with the sign of the cross as they enter church?

4:3 | Orthodox churches

KEY QUESTION

WHAT ARE THE
ICONOSTASIS
AND ICONS
AND WHY ARE
THEY SUCH AN
IMPORTANT
PART OF
WORSHIP IN
AN ORTHODOX
CHURCH?

The Roman Catholic Church, the Orthodox Church and the Anglican Church form the three great Christian 'families'. The 'family' with which people in this country are least familiar is that of the Orthodox Church although Orthodox Christians claim that their Church goes back to the earliest days of Christianity. The main reason for this unfamiliarity is that there are comparatively few Orthodox churches in Britain. The majority of them are found in Eastern Europe, Russia, and on the eastern side of the Mediterranean Sea. Altogether there are about 150 million Orthodox believers in the world.

Orthodox churches

Of all Christian churches Orthodox places of worship rely most heavily upon symbolism. The basic plan for each church is that of a square with a dome rising above the centre. This reminds all worshippers that everything in God's universe is orderly and correct. The square shape encourages people to realise that everyone in God's world is equal. The four corners of the square represent the four Gospels whilst the dome symbolises the heavens and the floor the earth. In the larger Orthodox buildings a painting of Christ the Pantocrator [ruler of the heavens, the universe and the earth] is stretched out across the ceiling.

The other features to note are:

1] The Iconostasis The High Altar, as with Roman Catholic and Anglican churches, is located in front of the east wall of the building. When the priest is facing the altar he has his back to the people. Behind him is a wooden screen, the iconostasis, which is a spiritual symbol of the great gulf that exists between almighty God and sinful human beings. The Royal Doors are in the centre of the iconostasis. Only the clergy are allowed to go through them and enter directly into the presence of God at the altar. This they do when they are preparing the bread and the wine for the Holy Liturgy.

The iconostasis is covered with icons [holy pictures]. The icon on the left shows the incarnation [birth] of Jesus whilst the one on the right portrays the promised return of Jesus to the earth. Between them they encompass the whole of sacred history. During the Holy Liturgy [see 5.7] the communion bread and wine are brought from the altar to the people in the church through the Royal Doors. The people are told that Jesus is present with them as they look back to his life on earth and forward to his future return on the clouds of heaven.

[A] What do you think that Orthodox believers mean when they say that icons are an earthly copy of a heavenly image?

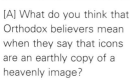
In the Glossary

Altar ~ Anglican Church ~ Apostle ~ Gospel ~ Holy Liturgy ~ Icon ~ Iconostasis ~ Orthodox Church ~ Roman Catholic Church ~ Saint ~ Virgin Mary

2] Icons You can see several icons in A. Icons are a very important ingredient in all Orthodox worship, whether in church or at home. Orthodox Christians believe that the all-powerful God is totally beyond human reach so making worship impossible without divine assistance. That is where icons come in. Icons are special religious paintings that bring God within human reach. As such they are used as devotional aids both in the church and home. Each icon is believed to be an earthly copy of a heavenly image and so the painting of it requires a high level of skill and religious devotion. Icon painters receive extensive training and they paint within an atmosphere of prayer and love for God.

Icons usually depict saints, Jesus, the Virgin Mary or the apostles. There are icons on the walls of Orthodox buildings and worshippers light candles in front of them. They then kiss the icon, or prostrate themselves in front of it, before taking

their seat in church. Some icons are thought to have had a miraculous history, being made 'without hands' or to have been transported from a far country. Sometimes miracles are associated with them.

 Talk it over

Why do you think that a prayerful attitude of mind is necessary before one can produce an acceptable icon? What does that suggest about the relationship between God, the painter and the icon produced?

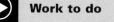 **Work to do**

1 a. What is an iconostasis?
b. Why is an iconostasis an important feature of an Orthodox church?
c. What is symbolised by an iconostasis?

2 a. What is an icon?
b. What makes an icon different from every other form of painting?
c. How do people often show their respect for an icon when they are in an Orthodox church?
d. Why do you think that icons are very important to Orthodox believers in their worship?

3 Imagine yourself to be an Orthodox Christian. Try to explain to a friend why the symbolism that surrounds you in church is important because it makes it possible for you to worship God.

[B] How is the whole of Christian history brought together on the iconostasis?

4:4 | Anglican churches

Traditional cross-shaped Anglican churches are to be found in most villages and towns in England. In the past these churches have fulfiled two important social functions in the community:

1] They provided consecrated ground in which members of the community were buried. Although a few of these burial-grounds linked to parish churches are still used the majority of them are full.

2] Their bells not only called people to worship each Sunday but were also used to announce important local, national and international events in an age before radio and television.

Inside Anglican churches

The older Anglican churches in this country were taken over from the Roman Catholics at the time of the Reformation, in the 16th century, by King Henry VIII. Not surprisingly, therefore, there is a close similarity between older Anglican and Roman Catholic church buildings. Amongst the features that most of them have in common are:

1] The Font The font is likely to be found just inside most churches since it was traditionally believed that infant baptism was the door into the Church. The water for this sacrament is kept in the font. People gather around the stone font for the service of infant baptism. Modern Anglican churches, though, often prefer to use a mobile font which can be placed in the middle of the church and people. This gives a modern emphasis to infant baptism providing the opportunity for the church as a whole to welcome a new baby into its spiritual family.

2] The Pulpit This is a stone platform to one side of the chancel. The priest climbs up into the pulpit to deliver his sermon to the people. The Anglican Church is a Reformed Church and this means it places a strong emphasis on the preaching of the Bible - although not as strong as other Protestant Churches. The focal-point in most Anglican churches is the altar since it is there that the sacrament of the Eucharist is celebrated. The Anglican Church, as the Roman Catholic and

[A] Which features can you recognise in this Anglican church?

1 What were the two main functions that the parish church played in towns and villages in the past?

2 Describe the part played by the following in worship in an Anglican church:
a. The font.
b. The pulpit.
c. The lectern.
d. The altar.

3 a. How has the position of the altar changed in modern Anglican churches?
b. What change in emphasis in belief is reflected in these changes?

Talk it over

Why do you think it is important
that changes in belief are reflected in
changes in the church building?

Find out

Try to find out more about the differences in
the Anglican Church between those who are
High Church and those who are Evangelicals.
Invite an Anglican priest in who would be able
to explain the differences between the two
groups to you. Find out how these differences
are likely to be reflected in the way that a
church is organised and decorated.

Orthodox Churches, is a sacramental Church.

3] The Lectern Normally made of wood or stone,
the lectern is a reading desk to one side of the altar
from which the Bible is read during a service. The
lectern often has a carving of an eagle on the front.
This is a reminder to the people of the words of
the prophet Isaiah in the Old Testament who said
that those who hope in the Lord 'will soar on
wings like an eagle' [Isaiah 40.31]. In High Church
[Anglo-Catholic] services the Gospel reading in
each service is given by the priest from the middle
of the congregation but the other readings are
given from the lectern.

4] The Altar The altar is the focal-point in all
Anglican, Roman Catholic and Orthodox
churches. In Anglo-Catholic Anglican churches the
altar is similar to that found in Roman Catholic
buildings with several candles and a crucifix. In
Low Church Anglican [Evangelical] churches,
however, there is usually little more than a cross, a
Bible and some flowers on the altar. Usually altars
are made of stone and found at the far end of the
church against the east wall. In modern Anglican
churches, however, there is sometimes a simple
wooden altar or communion table in the middle
of the church which the people gather around for
the service. In other churches the table is placed to
stand in front of the sanctuary. This is a common
feature in Evangelical churches. These changes mark
a shift of emphasis amongst Anglicans in belief:

   a. Traditionally the Eucharist, which takes place
   at the altar, has been seen as a sacrifice which
   the priest offers up to God on behalf of the
   people. The holiness of God was conveyed to

the people by the remoteness of the altar and
the priest. The priest faced the altar with his
back to the people.

   b. Many Anglicans now see the Eucharist as a
   fellowship meal in which everyone shares. For
   them the altar represents the table on which
   Jesus shared his last meal with his disciples. The
   altar, with the priest behind it, faces the
   congregation.

[B] Where would you
be likely to find a font in
an Anglican church - and
why?

In the Glossary

Altar ~ Anglican Church ~ Anglo-Catholic ~
Bible ~ Disciple ~ Eucharist ~ Evangelical
~ Font ~ Infant Baptism ~ Nonconformist
Church ~ Old Testament ~ Priest ~ Pulpit
~ Roman Catholic Church ~ Sanctuary

4:5 | Nonconformist Churches

KEY QUESTION

HOW DO
NONCONFORMIST
CHURCHES
DIFFER FROM
THOSE OF
OTHER
CHRISTIAN
DENOMINATIONS?

Some Nonconformist Churches, such as the Baptist Church and the Quakers, began in the 17th century. It was the preaching of John Wesley throughout Great Britain that led to the birth of the Methodist Church in the 18th century. His brother, Charles, wrote over 1,000 hymns and many of these are still used in Christian worship today. The 19th century saw the beginning of the Salvation Army. Most Nonconformist places of worship were built between the 17th and 19th centuries and have many features in common.

Different names

Many Nonconformist places of worship, especially in Wales, are called 'chapels'. These are small, and simple, churches. Quakers gather for regular worship in 'meeting-houses' since George Fox, their founder, wanted to put some distance between Quakers and other Churches. Meeting-houses are simple buildings with the chairs arranged around a table in the middle of the room. A Bible and other devotional books are placed on the table together with some flowers. The Salvation Army calls its places of worship 'citadels'. Citadels were places of refuge and security offering safety to those who feared for their lives. The Salvation Army citadel was intended to be a place of spiritual refuge, a place of security and safety from the wicked world around for those who needed its protection. Citadels are similar to other Nonconformist places of worship but they do not have a communion table or a pulpit. Neither the Salvation Army nor the Quakers celebrate Holy Communion, Infant Baptism or any of the other sacraments.

[A] A Methodist church. Who founded the Methodist Church and when?

(?) Find out

Find out as much as you can about any Nonconformist place of worship close to you. Write up some notes about the building, and what goes on there, in your folder.

Features

There are several features which are common to most, if not all, Nonconformist places of worship:
1] Whilst the emphasis in Anglican and Roman Catholic churches is on celebrating the sacraments, in Nonconformist churches [e.g Baptist, Methodist and United Reformed churches] it is on the preaching of the Word of God [the Bible]. There is no altar in a Nonconformist church but the focus is on the pulpit from which the sermon is preached. The sermon is the most important part of a Nonconformist service and it lasts longer than it does in other Churches.
2] Although Nonconformist Churches do not celebrate the sacraments as such they do celebrate the Breaking of Bread, a service sometimes called

All Nonconformist places of worship are simple in design. Why do you think that some find that this makes it easier for them to worship God?

1 Which Christian Churches worship:
a. In a chapel?
b. In a meeting-house?
c. In a citadel?

2 The Salvation Army calls its places of worship 'citadels'. Why are they called by this name?

3 a. What is the focal-point in a Nonconformist church?
b. Why?
c. What takes place at the communion table?
d. What is the mercy-seat?

the 'Lord's Supper' [see 5.8]. The bread and wine are laid out for this on the communion table which stands at the front of the church. The church leaders, including the minister and the elders, sit behind the table facing the congregation for the service.

3] Singing plays a very important part in Nonconformist worship. In some churches this is still led by an organ but in many others the organ has been replaced by a piano or keyboard. In a Salvation Army citadel the singing is likely to be led by a brass band. Many new religious songs been written recently and these are often led in church by a music-group. Everyone is encouraged to feel involved in the act of worship by singing together.

4] Baptist churches believe strongly in the baptism

of adults by full immersion [see 6.3]. For this purpose there is a baptismal pool [the baptistry] beneath the floor-boards at the front of most Baptist churches. This is filled with water each time a baptismal service is held whilst, at other times, the pool is emptied and covered. Occasionally other churches, such as the Anglican church, hold an adult baptism service in the local Baptist church.

5] Citadels are divided into two parts:
a. The Upper Area. This is the rostrum where the band sits. At the front of this there is a ledge from which an officer leads the service.
b. The Lower Area. This is where the people sit. The 'mercy-seat' is a long bench in front of the people. Anyone can come forward and kneel at this bench if they want to ask God's forgiveness or simply pray during the service. Each Salvation Army citadel also has a flag, the only Church to do so, and this is prominently displayed in the building along with the Army crest.

 In the Glossary

Altar ~ Anglican Church ~ Baptist Church ~ Bible ~ Breaking of Bread ~ Citadel ~ Holy Communion ~ Lord's Supper ~ Minister ~ Nonconformist Church ~ Quakers ~ Roman Catholic Church ~ Sacrament ~ Salvation Army

[B] The Salvation Army flag and motto are prominently displayed in all services. Why do you think that this is thought to be important?

4:6 | Christian Worship

KEY QUESTION

WHAT IS CHRISTIAN WORSHIP AND HOW IS IT EXPRESSED IN THE DIFFERENT CHURCHES?

Although Christians pray to God for help God always remains unknowable, a mystery to them. God is beyond human understanding and so any language about him can only, at best, be barely adequate. Most of the words and music which Christians use in their worship emphasise this side of God's character. Yet worship does go some way towards bridging the gulf between God and human beings. The hymns, the Bible readings, the prayers and the sermon are all designed to bring God closer to those who are worshipping.

Patterns of worship

Two broad styles of Christian worship are found in the Christian Church:

1] The liturgical style This follows a set pattern of words [a liturgy] which is laid down in a Prayer Book. Traditionally Anglicans have followed the Book of Common Prayer of 1661 although this has been replaced in many churches since 1980 by the modern Alternative Service Book. The liturgy of the Roman Catholic Church is laid down in the Missal. In these liturgical services the emphasis is upon familiar words and familiar actions. Neither of them change.

[A] Many people believe that a church service brings them into contact with God. Do you agree with them?

2] The non-liturgical style The approach of most Protestant Churches towards worship is different. Nonconformist churches do not have a Prayer Book but believe that their services are open to the leading of the Holy Spirit. The emphasis in these services is upon hymn-singing; prayers that follow no set pattern of words; readings from the Bible and the sermon. Although most Nonconformist Churches do offer Holy Communion and baptism these are not as important as they are in liturgical churches. The emphasis is very much upon the spoken word – the Word of God. Preaching and the teaching of the Bible are at the heart of all Protestant worship since it is through them that people can come to faith in Christ.

Charismatic worship

The Charismatic Movement grew out of the main Christian denominations in the 1960s. The movement is undenominational and is influential in the Anglican, Roman Catholic and Nonconformist Churches. It is based on the belief that the gifts of the Holy Spirit to the Church today still include prophecy; the ability to speak

---

BOX 1

1 CORINTHIANS 12.27-31

Now you are the body of Christ, and each one of you is part of it. And in the Church God has appointed first of all apostles, second prophets, third teachers, then workers of miracles, also having gifts of healing, those able to help others, those with gifts of administration, and those speaking in different kinds of tongues. Are we all apostles? Are we all prophets? Are we all teachers? Do all work miracles? Do all have the gift of healing? Do all speak in tongues? Do all interpret? Eagerly desire the greater gifts.

and pray in an unknown language [the gift of tongues] and the power to heal the sick. People receive these gifts individually when they are 'filled with the Holy Spirit', a highly emotional experience also known as 'the baptism of the Spirit'.

People are expected to use the gifts they have been given by God for the spiritual blessing of the church as a whole. Charismatic worship provides them with the opportunity to do this. In this worship the people:

- often raise their hands upwards to God as they pray;
- sing, dance, clap and embrace one another as they worship God;
- pray just as the Holy Spirit puts the words into their heads and mouths;
- speak in tongues; prophesy and see others healed.

Charismatic worship is mainly loud and exuberant.

Quaker worship

The contrast between the worship of charismatic Christians and that of Quakers [the Society of Friends] is very marked. Quakers come together in

their meeting-houses and spend most of their time worshipping in total silence. They believe that God speaks to each person through the 'inner voice' and that no-one can hear that voice unless they are listening silently. Occasionally someone might feel that God has spoken to them and that they should pass on that message to others. Having done so they then return to the silence of worship. When the meeting ends they shake hands in silence.

BOX 2

ARCHBISHOP DESMOND TUTU

We all have the need to worship… True Christian worship can never let us be indifferent to the needs of others, to the cries of the hungry, of the naked and homeless, of the sick and of the prisoners, of the oppressed and disadvantaged.

[B] A Quaker service is very different from other church services. What appeal do you think it has for some people?

▶ **Work to do**

1 a. What is liturgical worship?
b. Describe an example of this kind of worship.

2 a. What is non-liturgical worship?
b. Describe an example of this kind of worship.

3 What is different about charismatic worship?

4 a. Describe a Quaker meeting of worship.
b. Why do Quakers choose to worship God in this way?

4:7 | Prayer

Although prayer is a feature of all Christian services most Christians prefer to pray privately. Jesus encouraged them to do this by making it clear that prayer is largely a matter between God and the worshipper. *[Matthew 5.8]*. Jesus was adamant that prayer should not be offered to win the admiration of others but only to offer praise to God.

Three prayers

Three prayers are widely used in Christian worship:
1] The Lord's Prayer [the 'Our Father'] is the only Christian prayer which is commonly used across all denominations. Jesus gave this prayer [see box 1] to his disciples as a 'model' prayer for them to use and it contains the elements that should be present, in some shape or other, in all genuine Christian prayer:

a. Praise and adoration of God. Christian prayer begins with worshippers thanking God for the world that he has made and for the ability he has given them to enjoy it.

b. Confession. The confession of any sins committed and the seeking of God's forgiveness for them is an important ingredient of prayer.

c. Requests. Christians ask God to intervene in their own lives and in the lives of others. The prayers which are offered for other people are called 'intercessions'. They form an important part of all public and private prayer.

d. Thanksgiving. God is thanked for all his past goodness.

BOX 1

THE LORD'S PRAYER

This then is how you should pray: Our Father in heaven: May your holy name be honoured; may your kingdom come; may your will be done on earth as it is in heaven. Give us today the food we need. Forgive us the wrongs we have done, as we forgive the wrongs that others have done to us. Do not bring us to the hard testing, but keep us safe from the Evil One.

[A] Why do you think that Christians think that it is very important to teach their children to pray at an early age?

2] 'The Hail Mary' [the Ave Maria] is one of the most important Roman Catholic prayers and you can find it in box 2. Prayers to the Virgin Mary are offered in Roman Catholic and some Anglo-Catholic churches. Catholics believe that the Virgin Mary was taken up into heaven at the end of her life without dying. From this exalted position she is

Find out

Roman Catholics often pray to God through the Virgin Mary. Can you find out why they do this?

[B] What use do you think that Christians make of prayer throughout their lives?

able to 'intercede' with God on behalf of those who seek her help. The Hail Mary is a prayer of praise to the Virgin Mary whilst, at the same time, seeking her prayers to God in heaven.

3] The Jesus Prayer The Jesus Prayer is a form of prayer which consists of the repetition of the name of Jesus. The common form that it takes is: 'Lord Jesus Christ, Son of God, have mercy on me a sinner.' This prayer is commonly used by Orthodox Christians and goes back to the 6th century. In this short prayer, which is repeated over and over again, there are several important elements:

- the worship of Jesus;
- a confidence in the mercy of Jesus;
- a belief in the name of Jesus to deliver from all sin.

There are no set times for prayer – except in monastic life. Many Christians, though, choose to start each day with a 'Quiet Time' which involves study of a passage from the Bible and time spent praying.

Meditation and contemplation

Meditation is a way of praying which has its origins in the monastic movement. It involves deep concentration on the presence and activity of God. Meditation controls the mind and the breathing so that a person is left free to concentrate on God. The saints, especially the Virgin Mary, or passages from the Bible are used to help people to meditate. Contemplation goes a stage further. Through it a person becomes increasingly aware of the joy and beauty of God. In its most developed form contemplation leads to an experience of union with God. This experience, called 'absorption' or 'rapture', has been experienced by saints like Teresa of Avila and Julian of Norwich.

In the Glossary

Contemplation ~ Disciple ~ Hail Mary ~ Intercession ~ Jesus Prayer ~ Lord's Prayer ~ Meditation ~ Orthodox Church ~ Saint ~ Virgin Mary

Work to do

1 a. What is the Lord's Prayer?
   b. How do Christians use this prayer in their worship?

2 What do you think the following phrases in the Lord's Prayer mean:
a. 'Hallowed be thy name'?
b. 'Give us this day our daily bread'?
c. 'Deliver us from evil'?

3 Why do Christians pray?

BOX 2

THE HAIL MARY

Hail Mary, full of grace, the Lord is with thee. Blessed art thou among women and blessed is the fruit of thy womb, Jesus. Holy Mary, mother of God, pray for us sinners now and at the hour of our death. Amen.

4:8 | Aids to Prayer

The majority of Christians do not use any aids to help them to pray. In the Protestant Churches, for example, such aids are viewed with great suspicion. The teaching of the Reformation was that anyone can enter God's presence directly at any time. Other Christians, like Roman Catholics and Orthodox believers, find such aids very helpful in their religious lives. Amongst the aids most widely used are:

[A] How do you think that a person's familiarity with the feel of a rosary leaves them free to concentrate on the thoughts and prayers that it prompts them to utter?

A rosary

The rosary [A] is a traditional Roman Catholic aid to prayer. It is made up of five sets of ten beads each which are separated from each other by single beads. These are easily distinguishable to the touch. Attached to each single bead is a group of three further beads, another single bead and a cross or a crucifix. In using a rosary four prayers are involved:
1] The creed. The prayers start at the beginning of the rosary with the Creed.
2] The 'Our Father' [see 4.7] is said on the single bead.
3] A 'Hail Mary' [see 4.7] is said on each of the group of three beads.
4] The 'Gloria Patri' is said on the single bead which comes to the circle [see box 1].
For some Catholics fingering the beads in the rosary [rose-garden] is automatic. They use it to help them to contemplate fifteen holy 'mysteries' associated with the life of Jesus. These mysteries fall into three groups:
a. The 'Joyful' Mysteries These are events associated with early events in the Gospels including the Annunciation, Mary's visit to Elizabeth and the birth of Jesus.
b. The 'Sorrowful' Mysteries Events linked with the suffering and death of Jesus - the Garden of Gethsemane, the crowning with thorns, the carrying of the cross and the death itself.
c. The 'Glorious' Mysteries These include the resurrection and ascension of Jesus.
Like all forms of meditation, using the rosary is intended to lead the worshipper into a deeper experience of God.

BOX 1

THE GLORIA

Glory be to the Father, and to the Son and to the Holy Spirit. As it was in the beginning, is now and ever shall be, world without end. Amen.

An icon

Icons are religious paintings which are used as a help towards religious devotion by Orthodox Christians. There are icons both in the church and also in the home. They can be of Jesus, the Holy Family, the Virgin Mary or one of the saints of the Church. They are traditionally painted in egg tempera on wood but icons can also be made from metal, ivory or other materials. Often, in church, candles are placed in front of them. The

? **Find out**

The painting of icons is considered to be a vocation. Find out how the artists are trained and how they go about their work of producing icons which can be used by members of Orthodox churches to help them in their worship.

[B] Why do you think that candles play such an important part in Christian worship?

worshipper lights the candle and kisses the icon before taking their place for worship.

Crucifix

The cross is the main symbol of Christianity. A cross, in some shape or form, is likely to be found in the vast majority of churches. The crucifix is a

Work to do

1 Explain what use a Christian might make of the following in their praying:
a. A rosary. b. An icon. c. A crucifix.

2 a. What are votive candles?
b. Why might a Christian light one in a church?
c. Give another example of a time when a candle might be lit in a church.

3 Look at the Lord's Prayer and the Hail Mary in 4.7 and the Gloria in box 1. They are the most basic of all the prayers used by Roman Catholics. What link can you find between these three prayers?

cross which carries the figure of the dying Jesus. This symbolises the sufferings of Jesus by which Christians believe they are forgiven. Towards the end of Holy Week in many churches the crucifixes are empty to indicate the Christian belief that Jesus is no longer on the cross but has risen from the dead. Many Christians have crosses or crucifixes in their homes to help them to concentrate their minds on the death of Jesus. Often they pray in front of a crucifix and many Christians find it very moving to do this.

Votive candles

Votive candles are found in Roman Catholic churches [B]. The candles represent offerings which are made to God. On entering a church a Roman Catholic will light their votive candle and place it in a rack. At the same time they will make an offering or donation. The candle is the stimulus to make the 'offering' to God or the Virgin Mary. Traditionally the offering has been accompanied by a prayer for the restoration to health of the donor or someone else.

67

4:9 Using the Bible

The Bible is a great source of inspiration for Christian believers and it plays a very important part in:

Public worship

Passages from the Bible are read in almost all Christian services as well as providing the basis for sermons given by priests, ministers and lay-people. Both the Anglican and Roman Catholic Churches have a systematic programme for the public reading of most of the Bible over a given period of time - the readings are set down in a lectionary. In most services there are three readings from the Bible:
1] From the Old Testament.
2] From the Epistles [letters] of the New Testament.
3] From the Gospels.

The readings from the Old Testament and the Epistles are usually read by members of the congregation [lay-people]. The reading from the Gospels, however, is usually read by the priest to show its importance. In Roman Catholic, Orthodox and some High Anglican churches the Gospels are carried in procession to the middle of the church before the passage is read. The other readings, however, are given from the lectern.

The Gospel reading is isolated, and its importance underlined, because the Gospels contain the only record that we have of the birth, life, teaching, death and resurrection of Jesus. They are the foundation documents of the Christian faith. Whilst readings from any part of the Bible are spiritually valuable and nourishing they do not carry the authority, or the importance, which is attached to readings from the Gospels. Christians

[A] What do you think that Christians gain by reading a portion of the Bible each day on their own?

are, after all, followers of Jesus of Nazareth.

Sermons are also an important part of most church services although Protestants tend to attach a greater importance to them than other Churches. Most sermons are based on, or linked with, a passage from the Bible. In Protestant churches

---

BOX 1

HEBREWS 4.12,13

For the word of God is living and active. Sharper than any two-edged sword it penetrates even to dividing soul and spirit, joints and marrow; it judges the thoughts and attitudes of the heart. Nothing in all creation is hidden from God's sight. Everything is uncovered and laid bare before the eyes of him to whom we must give account.

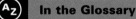 **In the Glossary**

Anglican Church ~ Bible ~ Christmas ~ Easter Day ~ Epistle ~ Evangelical ~ Gospel ~ Lent ~ Minister ~ Old Testament ~ Orthodox Church ~ Priest ~ Protestant ~ Roman Catholic Church

Some people believe that the Bible is the 'Word of God'. As such it must be believed, and obeyed, at all times. What kind of help and comfort do you think they might get from holding such a view?

1 Describe the different ways in which the Bible might be used in an act of Christian worship.

2 Explain why reading the Bible, in public and private, is an important part of Christian worship.

3 a. Why do the four Gospels have special importance for most Christians?
b. Choose one Christian festival and explain how it is based on events recorded in the Bible.

sermons can be given by lay-people as well as the clergy. In the sermon the preacher usually takes one of the Bible passages which has been read earlier in the service and explains both its meaning and its teaching for Christian life today.

Many churches also have regular mid-week meetings at which passages from the Bible are explained and studied. Some of these are closely linked with forthcoming festivals such as Christmas or Easter but often they are the opportunity for the priest or minister to work his or her way through books or themes of the Bible. Such Bible-studies are particularly a feature of Evangelical church life.

Personal Bible reading

Most Christians also spend time reading the Bible on their own. A familiarity with the Bible, and its contents, is seen as being very important if a person is to grow in their own Christian life. Study-notes are available, at different levels, to explain the passages and suggest ways in which the reading can be carried out systematically. Often Christians also meet together in small groups to study the Bible and discuss what it has to say.

Whenever Christians read the Bible, on their own or together, they are trying to understand what it says and to discover the relevance of its teaching for their own Christian lives.

BOX 2
ROMANS 15.4
For everything that was written in the past was written to teach us, so that through endurance and the encouragement of the Scriptures we might have hope.

[B] How do Christians show the importance of the Bible when they come together to worship?

4:10 | Christian Leaders

KEY QUESTION

WHAT ARE THE MAIN RESPONSIBILITIES OF PRIESTS OR MINISTERS WITHIN THEIR OWN CHURCHES TODAY?

The Quakers do not have full-time, paid leaders. People from the local group arrange, or preside over, worship in the meeting-house. In other churches widespread use is made of voluntary help [called 'lay leadership'] but the main responsibility for leading worship falls on the shoulders of priests [in the Roman Catholic, Anglican and Orthodox Churches] or ministers [in Nonconformist Churches].

Ordination

Each Church has its own ways of preparing its future priests or ministers but the training period is usually lengthy. It takes six years of training, for instance, before a Roman Catholic priest is considered ready to have responsibility for his own church. During this time the Church speaks of 'testing the vocation' of ordinands to see whether God has 'called' them to the work of the ministry. At the end of this time a Roman Catholic priest takes a vow of celibacy which is an acceptance that he will not marry or have sexual relations whilst he remains a priest. The Roman Catholic Church is the only one to demand this kind of commitment of its priests.

There is no suggestion in the New Testament that priests should be celibate. The requirement has been placed on Catholic priests, though, since the beginning of the 4th century. It is thought that the responsibilities of married, and family, life might cause a conflict with a priest's devotion to God and to the Church. In a sense, by being ordained, a priest, like a monk and a nun, becomes married to God.

During an ordination service in both the Roman Catholic and Anglican traditions the bishop lays his hands on each person being ordained. This is to give them God's Holy Spirit to help them in all the responsibilities, and challenges, that lie ahead. This also gives them the authority that they need to dispense the many sacraments to

BOX 1

IGNATIUS

Let everyone revere the deacons as Jesus Christ, the bishops as the image of the Father, and the presbyters [priests] as the senate of God and the assembly of the apostles. For without them one cannot speak of the Church.

[A] A Roman Catholic priest. How is the vocation of a Roman Catholic to the priesthood 'tested' before he is ordained?

the people *[see 5.1]*. Amongst these the Eucharist, which in the Roman Catholic Church is celebrated each day, is the most important. It is the priest alone who can give the bread and the wine, which to Roman Catholics become the body and blood of Jesus in the Mass, to the people. There are two exceptions in the Roman Catholic Church to the general rule that the priest alone can give the sacraments:

a. Any person can carry out infant baptism in an emergency.

b. In the Nuptual Mass, which ends the marriage service, the husband and the wife give the bread and wine of the Mass to each other.

In the Roman Catholic community the priest carries an authority not enjoyed by any other church leader. In Protestant Churches, such as Baptist and Methodist, the minister is mainly a preacher and a teacher.

Women priests

The Roman Catholic and Orthodox Churches do not ordain women priests. A letter, written by Pope John Paul II in 1994, ruled out the possibility of this ever happening in the Roman Catholic Church. At around the same time the first female priests were being ordained into the Church of England. Most Protestant Churches have ordained women for some time.

Those against the ordination of women point out that all the disciples of Jesus were male; that Paul was against women having any kind of public ministry and two thousand years of Church tradition have supported an all-male priesthood. Those who support the ordination of women argue that things have changed drastically since the time of Jesus and Paul and that women can bring many gifts to the work of a priest. This includes giving the sacraments; conducting services; visiting the old and sick; preparing people for baptism, confirmation and marriage; helping those who are bereaved and conducting funerals; running the parish and organising fund-raising activities.

BOX 2

THE BOOK OF COMMON PRAYER

A priest is called by God to work with the bishop and his fellow-priests, as servant and shepherd among the people to whom he is sent. He is to proclaim the word of the Lord, to call his hearers to repentance, and in Christ's name to absolve and to declare the forgiveness of sins. He is to baptise… He is to preside at the celebration of Holy Communion… He is to lead his people in prayer and worship… He is to minister to the sick and prepare the dying for death.

[B] What does the ordination service lead those who are entering the priesthood to expect?

 Work to do

1 Describe THREE tasks for which a priest takes responsibility.

2 What is the importance in the life of a Roman Catholic priest of celebrating the sacraments?

3 Why does the Roman Catholic Church insist on its priests being celibate?

4 'It doesn't matter whether a priest is male or female.' What are the main arguments for and against this point of view?

(A-Z) **In the Glossary**

Anglican Church ~ Baptism ~ Baptist Church ~ Bishop ~ Celibacy ~ Confirmation ~ Eucharist ~ Holy Spirit ~ Infant Baptism ~ Mass ~ Methodist Church ~ Minister ~ Monk ~ New Testament ~ Nonconformist Church ~ Nun ~ Ordination ~ Paul ~ Priest ~ Orthodox Church ~ Quaker ~ Roman Catholic Church ~ Sacrament

5:1 | The Sacraments

KEY QUESTION

WHAT ARE THE SACRAMENTS AND WHY ARE THEY IMPORTANT?

BOX 1

THE BOOK OF COMMON PRAYER

Q: *What meanest thou by the word Sacrament?*
A: *I mean an outward and visible sign of an inward and spiritual grace.*

The sacraments are at the very heart of the Christian faith for all Roman Catholic and Orthodox believers – and for many Anglicans as well. The sacraments have a much lower profile in Nonconformist Churches where they are not usually called sacraments. The sacraments are ceremonies which can be traced back either to Jesus or the early Church. Since then the sacraments ['mysteries'] have been used to transmit the mystery of the Christian faith to countless worshippers.

Two ingredients

There are two important ingredients to every sacrament:

1] The physical side This is the part of the sacrament that can be felt, touched, smelled, seen or tasted. During the Eucharist, for example, the worshipper drinks a small amount of wine and eats a little bread. By taking these the worshipper is sharing spiritually in the death of Jesus on the cross. Similarly, in infant baptism, water is poured over the baby's head to symbolise his or her cleansing from sin.

2] The spiritual side The physical elements in the sacraments are only important as symbols. The ceremonies which go with each sacrament have little value in themselves. Each sacrament is designed to bring a spiritual blessing to the person which could not be experienced in any other way.

The sacraments

Both the Roman Catholic and the Orthodox Church celebrate seven sacraments – although the Orthodox Church prefers to call them 'Mysteries'. They are:

1] The Eucharist [5.4-5.8] – the most important sacrament. This sacrament carries different names in the various Churches – as you will see in 5.4.
2] Infant Baptism [6.1] – the sacrament of initiation into the Church showing the symbolic cleansing of the young child from his or her sin.
3] Confirmation [6.2] – the sacrament by which a person enters into full membership of the Church.
4] Penance [5.3] – the sacrament which offers the confession and full forgiveness of sins.
5] Reconciliation [Extreme Unction. 5.2] – the

[A] A priest in the Church of England baptises a baby. Why do you think that almost all Churches believe that it is important to introduce children to the Christian faith as early as possible?

(A-Z) In the Glossary

Anglican Church ~ Baptist Church ~ Breaking of Bread ~ Confirmation ~ Eucharist ~ Holy Communion ~ Holy Liturgy ~ Holy Orders ~ Infant Baptism ~ Mass ~ Orthodox Church ~ Penance ~ Priest ~ Protestant ~ Quakers ~ Roman Catholic Church ~ Sacrament ~ Salvation Army ~ Trinity

Find out

Find out why the Salvation Army and
the Quakers do not celebrate any of
the sacraments. Write up your notes
into your folder.

Talk it over

Someone has said that " sacraments are
the only way that God could bless us."
What do you think they meant?

anointing of the sick with oil, especially those
approaching death.

6] Holy Orders [4.10] - the consecration of a
person as a deacon, a priest or a bishop.

7] Matrimony [6.4] - marriage in which the
husband and wife offer the Eucharist to each
other.

Most Protestant Churches only recognise two
sacraments - the Eucharist and baptism. These are
the only ones that can be traced with certainty
back to the ministry of Jesus. Whilst most churches
baptise infants the Baptist Church will only baptise
believing adults. The Salvation Army and the
Quakers, alone among Protestant Churches, do not
include any sacraments in their worship.

The importance
of the sacraments

Most Christians believe that Jesus demonstrated the
power of God through his actions and teachings
when he was on earth. Now, that same divine
power reaches them through the sacraments. This
belief is most important in those Churches, like the
Roman Catholic Church, which describe
themselves as 'sacramental'. In these churches the
main role of the priest is to administer the
sacraments - which he alone can do. They believe
that, through the sacraments, human beings can

gain some understanding of the relationship which
exists between God the Father, God the Son and
God the Holy Spirit - the Trinity.

[B] Jesus meets with his
disciples for his last meal.
The Eucharist is based
on this meal. Why do you
think that many Christians
only celebrate the
sacraments that can be
linked directly with the
ministry of Jesus?

BOX 2

THE CATECHISM OF
THE CATHOLIC CHURCH

*The purpose of the sacraments is to sanctify
[make holy] men, to build up the Body of
Christ [the Church] and, finally, to give
worship to God. Because they are signs they
also instruct. They not only pre-suppose faith
but by words, and objects, they also nourish,
strengthen and express it. That is why they
are called the sacraments of faith.*

Work to do

1 a. What is a sacrament?
b. What is the physical side of a
sacrament and why is it important?
c. What is the purpose of a sacrament?

2 a. How many sacraments are
recognised by the Roman Catholic and
Orthodox Churches?
b. How many sacraments are recognised by
most Protestant Churches?
c. Which two Protestant Churches do not
celebrate any of the sacraments?

3 a. List the seven sacraments celebrated
by Roman Catholic and Orthodox
believers.
b. Write a ONE sentence definition of each
of them.

5:2 | Anointing the Sick

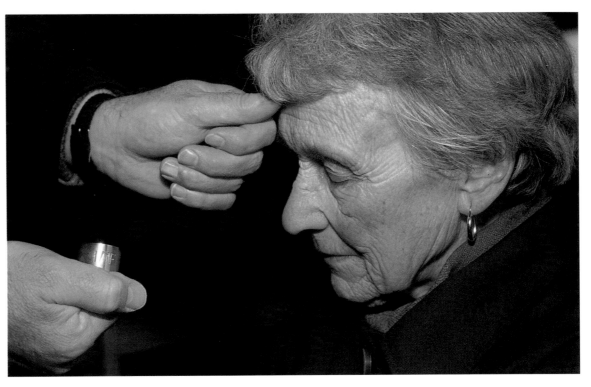

[A] Where does the oil
come from that is used
for anointing?

Anointing sick people with oil is one of the seven sacraments performed regularly in
the Roman Catholic Church. It offers the sick person the comfort of knowing
that they are not alone in their illness – God is with them. It also encourages
them to take comfort in the knowledge that the Christian community, the Church, is
praying for them.

The sacrament of anointing

The practice of anointing the sick with oil and
asking God to heal them goes back to the New
Testament – see box 1. As James makes clear,
though, it is the prayer of believing people to God,
rather than the anointing, which brings healing to
the person. There are three main stages to the
sacrament as it is practiced today in the Catholic
Church:

1] The priest sprinkles the sick person, and
everyone present, with holy water. This water is a

 In the Glossary

Bishop ~ Diocese ~ Gospels ~ Holy Communion
~ Holy Spirit ~ Lord's Prayer ~ Maundy Thursday ~
New Testament ~ Priest ~ Roman Catholic Church
~ Sacrament ~ Viaticum

reminder that the person began to follow Jesus and
became a member of the Christian community
when they were baptised as a baby. Now at the end
of their life, through their suffering, they are
sharing in the sufferings that Jesus himself
experienced. Bible readings and prayers follow

1 What does the Christian Church do to help the sick?

2 Explain ONE way in which a Christian might help a person cope with suffering - and death.

3 a. What does the word 'viaticum' mean?
b. What is the 'viaticum'?
c. What does the viaticum try to assure a person about?

4 The sacrament of anointing the sick falls into three stages. Describe why each of them is important.

5 Read the quotation in box 1.
a. What is it that will save the sick person?
b. How is the possible link between sickness and sin explained in this passage?

which ask God to forgive the sick person for their sins. The priest then lays his hands on the head of the person reminding them that Jesus often did this before he healed a person in the Gospels.

2] The priest anoints the forehead of the sick person with olive oil. As he does so he says: 'Through this holy anointing may the Lord in his love and mercy help you with the grace of the Holy Spirit.' He then anoints the hands of the person saying the words: 'May the Lord who frees you from sin save you and raise you up.'

The oil being used in the sacrament has been blessed by the bishop in a special service held in the cathedral of the diocese every Maundy Thursday. Whenever it is used in a sacrament oil is always the symbol of God's healing and strength. The priest says a prayer in which the condition of the sick person is mentioned. The 'Our Father' [the Lord's Prayer] is said as this prayer speaks of all human needs and conditions. In particular, it reminds the sick person of a loving heavenly Father who cares for and protects all of his children. Whatever happens, the person can be sure that God will always be with them. No Christian faces sickness or death alone.

3] The sacrament of anointing the sick is combined with the giving of the bread and wine of Holy Communion. This unites the sick person with God in a special and unique way. As the host [bread] is held up so the priest invites everyone present to trust in God's great love.

BOX 1

JAMES 5.13-16

Is any one of you in trouble? He should pray. Is anyone happy? Let him sing songs of praise. Is any one of you sick? He should call the elders of the church to pray over him and anoint him with oil in the name of the Lord. And the prayer offered in faith will make the sick person well; the Lord will raise him up. If he has sinned he will be forgiven. Therefore confess your sins to each other and pray for each other so that you may be healed. The prayer of a righteous man is powerful and effective.

The viaticum

If the person receiving Holy Communion is dying then the bread and the wine are called the 'viaticum' [food for the journey]. The viaticum is offered in the belief that it will be the last sacrament the person receives on earth. The journey about to begin is the passage from earthly life through death to eternal life. The person is reminded of their baptismal vows and assured that they are following in the footsteps of Jesus and travelling to their Father in heaven. The kiss of peace is exchanged by everyone at the viaticum. Death is the completion and crown of all human life on earth. They are now following their Lord to eternal glory and the banquet which all the faithful will enjoy in God's kingdom.

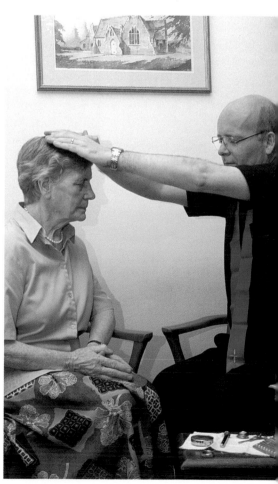

[B] Why does the priest lay his hands on the head of the sick person?

5:3 | The Sacrament of Reconciliation

KEY QUESTION

WHAT IS THE SACRAMENT OF RECONCILIATION AND WHY IS IT AN IMPORTANT PART OF CHRISTIAN WORSHIP?

The sacrament of reconciliation is used in Roman Catholic and many Anglican churches. It is a sacrament that recognises a basic human need. A person becomes a member of the Christian community through baptism and confirmation. This, though, is only the beginning of a lengthy process in their spiritual journey. Human beings are always prone to sin and, sometimes, this is a very heavy burden for them to carry. To help them to find forgiveness for their sins, and release from the burden of guilt, the Church offers the sacrament of reconciliation.

Penance - the old way

The Roman Catholic Church has offered the sacrament of penance for centuries. In the 17th century 'confessional boxes' were built in Catholic churches so that people could confess their sins to a priest in secret. The priest sat on one side of an iron grille [A] and the penitent on the other. The identity of the person confessing was kept secret. After confessing their sin the person was given a penance [penalty] to carry out and then given absolution [God's forgiveness]. The priest was bound by the 'seal of confession' which meant that he could not reveal anything said in the confessional to anyone else.

Confession - the new way

In some churches there is still a confessional box which is used regularly. The Second Vatican Council [1962-65] of the Roman Catholic Church, however, opened up a new way which allowed the priest and the penitent to sit talking to each other [B]. This allows the person to receive more direct help and counselling from the priest. The priest, though, is still bound by the confidentiality of the 'seal of confession'.

Confessing sins

In the act of confessing sins the following happens:
1] The penitent is reminded by the priest that God will always forgive the person who is genuinely

[A] Why do you think that the Second Vatican Council made some changes in the confessional?

BOX 1

ABSOLUTION PRONOUNCED BY THE PRIEST AFTER CONFESSION

God, the Father of mercies, through the death and resurrection of his Son had reconciled the world to himself and sent the Holy Spirit among us for the forgiveness of sins; through the ministry of the Church may God give you pardon and peace, and I absolve you from your sins in the name of the Father, and of the Son and of the Holy Spirit.

Talk it over

Why do you think that it is important for someone to make a firm commitment to change their way of life before they can receive forgiveness?

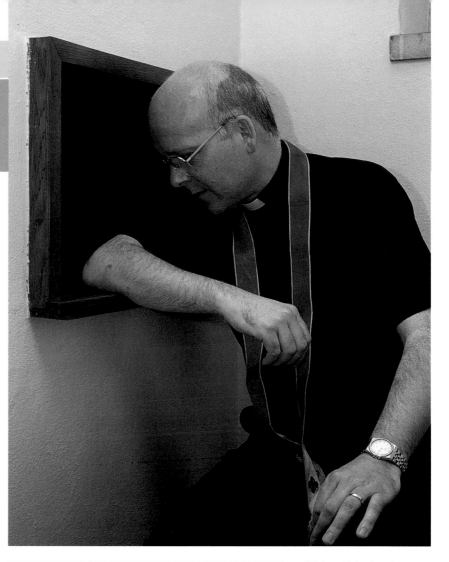

[B] In which churches would you be likely to see a scene like this?

sorry for their sins. The priest reads a passage from the Bible to the person to emphasise this.

2] When the penitent has confessed their sin the priest offers a few words of encouragement and advice. He then suggests a penance, such as the saying of a few prayers, so that the person can show God that they are genuinely sorry.

3] Once confession has been made and the penance accepted then an 'act of sorrow' must take place. God's forgiveness is only available to those people who show that they are really sorry for the sins of the past [contrition] and ready to make sure that the sin is not repeated [a purpose of amendment].

4] The priest then uses the authority given to him by God and the Church to assure the person that they have been forgiven. This he does by placing his hands on the penitent or by raising his right hand as he pronounces the absolution. The sign of the cross is made over the person as the priest says: 'I absolve you from your sins in the name of the Father, and of the Son and of the Holy Spirit. 'This assures the person that it is through the death of Jesus on the cross that he or she has been forgiven. It also restores to the person that sense of forgiveness and acceptance that they were given through their baptism.

> **BOX 2**
>
> **THE CATECHISM OF THE CATHOLIC CHURCH**
>
> *Sin is an offence against God, a rupture of communion with him. At the same time it damages communion with the Church.*

In the Glossary

Absolution ~ Anglican Church ~ Baptism ~ Bible ~ Confirmation ~ Penance ~ Priest ~ Roman Catholic Church ~ Sacrament of Reconciliation ~ Sacrament

Work to do

1 Read the absolution that the priest pronounces on those who confess their sins in box 1.

a. What is absolution?

b. What does a person need to do before the priest can pronounce the absolution?

c. Why is it particularly appropriate to speak to God as 'the Father of mercies' in the absolution?

d. How has God shown that he is willing to forgive the sins of those who confess them?

e. What part does the Church play in the process of forgiving?

2 Describe carefully the events that lead up to the priest pronouncing the forgiveness of sins on a person.

3 Look at the definition of sin in box 2. This definition is taken from the Catechism of the Catholic Church. How would you define 'sin'?

Read Luke 22.7-23

5:4 | Holy Communion

WHY IS THE SERVICE OF HOLY COMMUNION AT THE HEART OF MOST ACTS OF CHRISTIAN WORSHIP?

For the majority of Christians Holy Communion, or the Eucharist, is the most important act of worship in which they take part. Holy Communion means 'holy sharing' and refers to the service in which Christians share bread and wine with each other – and with God. As they do so they also share spiritually in the death of Jesus on the cross [A].

In the beginning

It is the clear link between Holy Communion and the life of Jesus [box 1] that gives this sacrament a unique place in the Church's worship. From the Day of Pentecost onwards members of the early Church met together to 'break bread' because they were sure that Jesus had told them to do so – see box 2. All four Gospels and one of the epistles [1.Corinthians 11] record what happened when Jesus shared his last meal with his disciples. We are told that, on the night on which he was betrayed, Jesus took a loaf of bread, broke it, and gave a piece to each of his disciples with the words: 'Take and eat. This is my body.' Moments later he took a goblet of wine and passed it around amongst his friends, saying to them: "Drink it, all of you… this is my blood, which seals God's covenant, my blood poured out for many for the forgiveness of sins."

[Matthew 26.26-28].

These words form the basis of the service of Holy Communion today.

Many names

Throughout the history of the Church Christians have disagreed about the precise meaning of this service. These differences are reflected in the different names which the service carries:

1] The Eucharist In the Anglican Church the service of Holy Communion is usually called 'the Eucharist ['Thanksgiving'] [See 5.5].

2] The Mass In the Roman Catholic Church the service is called the Mass, probably from the final words of the old Latin service – 'Ita Missa Est' ['Go, it is finished'] [See 5.6].

3] The Holy Liturgy This is the name given

BOX 1

LUKE 22.19-20

He took bread, gave thanks and broke it, and gave it to them, saying, 'This is my body given for you; do this in remembrance of me.' In the same way, after supper he took the cup, saying, 'This cup is the new covenant in my blood, which is poured out for you.'

[A] Why do you think that Jesus left such everyday objects as bread and wine to help people celebrate his death?

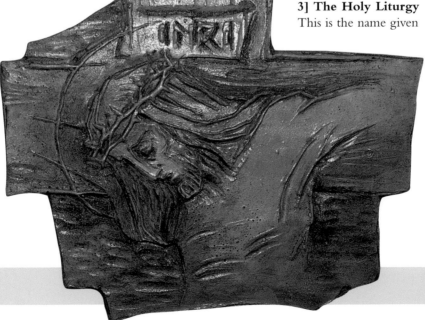

BOX 2

1 CORINTHIANS 11.23-25

For I received from the Lord what I also passed on to you: The Lord Jesus, on the night he was betrayed, took bread, and when he had given thanks, he broke it and said, 'This is my body, which is for you; do this in remembrance of me.' In the same way, after supper he took the cup, saying: 'This cup is the new covenant in my blood, do this, whenever you drink it, in remembrance of me.'

Anglican Church ~ Breaking of Bread ~ Day of
Pentecost ~ Disciple ~ Epistle ~ Eucharist
~ Gospel ~ Holy Communion ~ Holy Liturgy ~
Last Supper ~ Lord's Supper ~ Mass ~ Orthodox
Church ~ Priest ~ Protestant ~ Roman Catholic
Church ~ Sacrament ~ Transubstantiation

1 a. What do the bread and wine at a Holy Communion service represent?

b. Give TWO other names by which the service of Holy Communion is known.

c. Explain what it is that makes Holy Communion unique amongst the sacraments celebrated in the Christian Church.

2 Explain the link between the last meal that Jesus shared with his disciples and the service of Holy Communion.

3 Why is the Eucharist often described by Christians as a service of 'holy communion?

4 Read box 2 carefully. Twice the followers of Jesus are told to act 'in remembrance of me'. What are they actually being told to do?

to the service in Orthodox churches. The 'liturgy' is a traditional order of service and that used in the Holy Liturgy goes back, unchanged, to the 4th century *[See 5.7]*.

4] The Breaking of Bread [The Lord's Supper] The Gospels tell us that Jesus 'broke bread' with his disciples at the Last Supper whilst the phrase 'the Lord's Supper' is taken from the writings of Paul. Nonconformists use either of these titles for their service of Holy Communion [See 5.8].

The meaning of Holy Communion

There is a real difference between the way that Roman Catholics/Orthodox Christians, on the one hand, and Protestants, on the other, understand Holy Communion. This difference has been at the heart of many bitter disputes in the past. The difference revolves around what happens to the bread and wine during the service:

1] Roman Catholic and Orthodox churches Christians from these Churches believe that Christ is really 'present' in the bread and wine. The bread and wine become the actual body and blood of Christ when they are 'consecrated' by the priest during the service. This belief is called 'transubstantiation'.

2] Protestant churches Most Anglicans and other Protestants believe that the service is largely one of remembrance by which those who eat the bread and drink the wine receive a spiritual blessing. Throughout the service the elements remain what they are – symbols which do not change.

Why do you think that, from the beginning, the Christian Church felt it necessary to celebrate the death of Jesus?

[B] Most Christians regularly celebrate Holy Communion - as Jesus told them to do. What spiritual benefit do you think they derive from doing so?

5:5 | The Eucharist

KEY QUESTION

WHAT IS DISTINCTIVE ABOUT THE WAY THAT ANGLICANS CELEBRATE THE EUCHARIST?

[A] How might different people in an Anglican congregation understand this action of the priest?

BOX 1

OPENING COLLECT. BOOK OF COMMON PRAYER

Almighty God, unto whom all hearts be open, all desires known, and from whom no secrets are hid, cleanse the thoughts of our hearts by the inspiration of thy Holy Spirit, that we may perfectly love thee, and worthily magnify thy holy name, through Christ, our Lord. Amen.

The frequency with which individual Anglican churches celebrate the Eucharist, the service of thanksgiving to God for the death of Jesus, indicates the importance which they attach to it. In Anglo-Catholic churches, for instance, the Eucharist is at the centre of all worship and takes place several times a week, if not daily. In Evangelical churches, however, the Eucharist is likely to be celebrated once on a Sunday and once more during the week. Many churches also celebrate the Eucharist on special festival days such as Ascension Day.

The Eucharist

The Alternative Service Book of the Church of England, published in 1980, emphasised that the Eucharist is a family meal in which every member of the church family is invited to share. This sharing aspect is underlined by the giving, and receiving, of the 'Peace' just before the moment when the bread and wine are shared. At this moment in the service the people shake hands, hug or kiss, while saying to each other 'The Peace of the Lord be with you.'

Once the priest has blessed the elements he or she invites everyone to share in the spiritual meal with the words: 'Draw near and receive the body of our Lord Jesus Christ, which was given for you, and his blood, which was shed for you. Take this in remembrance that Christ died for you, and feed on him in your hearts with thanksgiving.' The people then come forward and kneel at the chancel steps

(A-Z) In the Glossary

Altar ~ Alternative Service Book ~ Anglican Church ~ Anglo-Catholic ~ Ascension ~ Church of England ~ Eucharist ~ Evangelical ~ Priest ~ Protestant

Work to do

1 Explain why the Eucharist is such an important act of worship for Anglicans.

2 Describe a celebration of the Eucharist.

3 The Eucharist ends with the people being sent out into the world to serve God and the Gospel of Christ. Why do you think that this is an appropriate way to end the service?

4 a. What does it mean to call the Anglican Church a 'Broad Church'?
b. How might an Anglo-Catholic understand the Eucharist?
c. How might an Evangelical understand the Eucharist?

Talk it over

Why do you think that the giving, and receiving, of the Peace has become an important feature of a modern Eucharist service?

before the priest who says to each person, 'The body of Christ,' before handing them the bread. Then, as he hands them the goblet containing the wine, he says, 'The blood of Christ.' The person replies each time 'Amen [so be it].'

The spiritual food which the people have received gives them the strength, and the vision, to go out into the world to share the Gospel of Christ with others. The Anglican Eucharist and the Catholic Mass end on the same note.

The meaning of the Eucharist

The Anglican Church is often described as being 'a broad Church'. This means that its members hold many different beliefs and points of view whilst still belonging to the one Church. There are two broad ways of understanding the Eucharist and these very different opinions are reflected in most Anglican congregations. When people receive the

bread and the wine they understand its significance in their own way:

1] The High Church or Anglo-Catholic point of view. Many priests, and church members, hold a Catholic view of the Eucharist. They believe that, during the service, the bread and wine turn into the actual body and blood of Christ. Each time they celebrate the Eucharist the death of Christ is actually being re-enacted on the altar. You will find out more about this in 5.6.

2] The Low Church or Evangelical point of view. This coincides with the Protestant viewpoint which sees the Eucharist as a commemoration, a way of remembering the death of Jesus. The bread and wine are no more than symbols and they remain so throughout the service. Through them communicants are able to see a little of the love of God which was expressed in the life and death of Jesus. God, they believe, blesses them through celebrating the Eucharist in a way that does not happen in any other service. This is what makes the Eucharist so special.

[B] What does it mean to describe the modern Eucharist service as a 'family meal'?

BOX 2

EUCHARISTIC PRAYER

Who in the same night that he was betrayed took bread and gave you thanks. He broke it and gave to his disciples, saying: Take, eat; this is my body which is given for you, do this in remembrance of me. In the same way, after supper he took the cup and gave thanks, he gave it to them, saying: Drink this, all of you; this is the blood of my new covenant, which is shed for you, and for many, for the forgiveness of sin. Do this, as often as you drink it, in remembrance of me.

5:6 | The Mass

KEY QUESTION

WHY IS THE
CELEBRATION
OF THE MASS
SO IMPORTANT
FOR ALL ROMAN
CATHOLICS?

Going to Mass and receiving the consecrated bread [called the 'host'] and wine at the altar are at the centre of every committed Roman Catholic's life. The Mass is celebrated daily in every Catholic church and members are under a spiritual obligation to go regularly – especially on holy days of obligation. The service is a regular renewal of faith as people listen to God speaking to them through the Bible, pray together and receive the body and blood of Jesus.

The liturgy

The liturgy that makes up the Mass is divided into two parts:

1] The liturgy of the Word Catholics believe that to participate fully in the Mass they must be cleansed from all their sins and this is where the service begins. To be cleansed from a major [mortal] sin a person must attend confession but forgiveness for lesser [venial] sins can be obtained through the 'penitential rite' with which the Mass

BOX 1

CATECHISM OF THE CATHOLIC CHURCH

In the Eucharist Christ gives us the very body which he gave up for us on the cross, the very blood which he 'poured out for many for the forgiveness of sins'. The Mass is so important for all Catholics because it is the means by which their spiritual lives are renewed day by day. Not only does the Mass unite Catholics with Jesus Christ but it also unites them with one another.

[A] Find out why Roman Catholics call the bread in the Mass a host.

starts. The people are invited to repent from their sins and seek God's forgiveness before being given absolution by the priest.

Three readings from the Bible – from the Old Testament, the Epistles and the Gospels – are read. The readings are taken from the Lectionary which outlines a three-year cycle of readings in the Gospels so that all of the four Gospels are read aloud during this period. The readings are followed by a sermon [the homily] in which the priest explains some aspect of the Christian life before leading the people in reciting the Nicene Creed. This is one of the great statements of Christian faith, dating from the 4th century, which sums up what the Church believes about God the Father, Jesus Christ, the Holy Spirit, the Church and the life to come. Prayers of intercession are then offered to seek God's blessing on the Church and on the world.

2] The liturgy of the Mass Members of the congregation bring forward the peoples' gifts of

Altar ~ Bible ~ Epistle ~ Holy Communion ~ Holy Spirit ~ Liturgy ~ Lord's Prayer ~ Mass ~ New Testament ~ Nicene Creed ~ Old Testament ~ Priest ~ Tabernacle ~ Transubstantiation

1 Read boxes 2 and 3 carefully.
a. What is said in box 2 about the death of Jesus which is celebrated each Mass?
b. Why, according to box 3. is the celebration of the Mass so important for all Catholics?

2 Describe a celebration of the Mass and explain why it is so important to Roman Catholics to attend Mass regularly.

3 a. What is transubstantiation?
b. How does the belief of Roman Catholics about the meaning of the Eucharist differ from the belief held by most Protestants?

4 What happens during:
a. The Liturgy of the Word?
b. The Liturgy of the Mass?

money, bread and wine. This underlines that the Mass is the sacrifice of the people as well as the sacrifice of Jesus. After the priest has washed his hands at the altar he says the Eucharistic prayer [see box 1] which combines the needs of the people with the sacrifice of Jesus. This unending sacrifice is about to be offered on the altar. The prayer of consecration then follows and it is at this point that the bread and wine become the actual body and blood of Jesus. A bell is rung to show that this has happened. The people reply 'Christ has died, Christ is risen, Christ will come again.'

The people then join together in the Lord's Prayer [the 'Our Father'] to pray for forgiveness and the provision of their everyday needs. Before sharing communion with each other they give the Peace as a demonstration of their love. The priest then takes the Holy Communion himself before distributing it to the people. Any remaining bread [hosts] are placed back in the tabernacle. These are used if communion is taken to a sick person in their home.

BOX 2

THE EUCHARISTIC PRAYER

Almighty God, we pray that your angel may take this sacrifice to your altar in heaven. Then as we receive from this altar the sacred body and blood of your Son, let us be filled with every grace and blessing.

BOX 3

PREFACE TO THE HOLY EUCHARIST

He [Christ] is the true and eternal priest who establishes this unending sacrifice. He offered himself as a victim for our deliverance and taught us to make this offering in his memory. As we eat his body which he gave for us, we grow in strength. As we drink his blood which is poured out for us, we are washed clean.

Finally the Mass ends as everyone is sent out into the world to help their neighbour, especially if that neighbour is in need. By serving others they are not only helping those in need but serving God as well. They are also strengthening their own spiritual lives and building on the help received through the Mass. The priest dismisses the congregation with the words 'Go in peace to love and serve the Lord.' In this way the Catholic Mass ends on the same note as the Eucharistic service in an Anglican church.

[B] Why do you think that the priest takes the wine and bread himself before offering it to the people?

5:7 | The Holy Liturgy

KEY QUESTION

WHAT IS THE SERVICE OF HOLY LITURGY AND WHAT SIGNIFICANCE DOES IT HAVE FOR THE ORTHODOX BELIEVER?

[A] The priest stands in front of the iconostasis. When might he do this during the Holy Liturgy?

In the Orthodox Church the Holy Liturgy is the service of Holy Communion. As in the Roman Catholic Mass the Liturgy is also divided into two parts:

1] THE LITURGY OF THE WORD The first part of the Holy Liturgy includes prayers, Bible readings and a sermon. Its climax comes with the 'Lesser Entrance' when the priest, carrying the book of the Gospels above his head, comes through the Royal Doors. Surrounded by attendants carrying candles the priest reads a passage from the Gospels before returning to the High Altar.

2] THE LITURGY OF THE FAITHFUL Most of the Liturgy of the Faithful is conducted by the priest behind the iconostasis [see A], a highly symbolic part of every Orthodox church. The iconostasis symbolises the enormous gulf which exists between God and human beings. This gulf is so great that only the priest is able to enter directly into God's presence, represented by the High Altar. People can glimpse the divine presence from a distance but they cannot draw any closer.

BOX I

THE NICENE CREED

We believe in one God, the Father, the almighty, maker of heaven and earth, of all that is seen and unseen. We believe in one Lord, Jesus Christ, the only Son of God, eternally begotten of the Father, God from God, Light from Light, true God from true God, begotten not made, of one Being with the Father. Through him all things were made. For us men and our salvation he came down from heaven; by the power of the Holy Spirit he became incarnate of the Virgin Mary and was made man. For our sake he was crucified under Pontius Pilate; he suffered death and was buried. On the third day he rose again according to the Scriptures; he ascended into heaven and is seated at the right hand of the Father. He will come in glory… We believe in the Holy Spirit… We believe in one holy catholic and apostolic church… We look for the resurrection from the dead… Amen.

The Liturgy of the Faithful begins with the priest preparing the bread and wine for communion [see B]. The Royal Doors are closed whilst this is going on to symbolise the holiness of the death of Jesus and of the elements of bread and wine which represent that death. The priest then makes the 'Greater Entrance' by passing through the Royal Doors carrying the bread and wine. The people bow as the procession passes. The priest returns to the altar and lays out the bread and wine. The people greet one another with the kiss of peace before reciting the Nicene Creed together [box 1]. In the prayers that follow, the story of the Last Supper is retold before everyone joins in the Lord's Prayer. Finally the priest raises the bread and breaks it – a part of the service called the 'elevation'. The choir sings and bells are rung.

The priest then stands in front of the Royal Doors and those receiving communion come

▶ **Work to do**

1 Describe the service of the Holy Liturgy in an Orthodox church dividing your answer into:
a. The Liturgy of the Word.
b. The Liturgy of the Faithful.

2 a. Describe the part played by the priest in the Orthodox Holy Liturgy.
b. Explain why the priest is given such a prominent part to play in the service.

3 Explain the meaning of the following terms from the Holy Liturgy:
a. The Lesser Entrance.
b. The Greater Entrance.
c. The Elevation.
d. The Antidoron.

? **Find out**

The holiness of God is a central element of Orthodox belief. How is this side of God's character emphasised in an Orthodox church?

forward and kneel. Each person receives a piece of bread dipped in wine which is placed at the back of their throat on a silver spoon. Some of the bread is not consecrated. This bread is broken into small pieces and is called the 'antidoron'. At the end of the service the people come forward to the priest and kiss a cross that he is holding. They share the unconsecrated bread as a sign of their fellowship and love – just as the early Christians shared their meals with one another.

The meaning

Two important points:

1] The Holy Liturgy is a beautiful service which engages all the senses – with its colourful vestments worn by the clergy, the clouds of incense that fill the air and its haunting, unaccompanied music. This beauty is a very important element in the meaning of the Holy Liturgy. It provides worshippers with a glimpse of what life is going to be like in heaven. It opens the doors of paradise a little to reveal a glimpse of God the Father, God the Son and the Holy Spirit.

2] The icons which can be seen everywhere in an Orthodox church are one of the keys to understanding the Holy Liturgy. Made according to holy traditions that go back for centuries the icons radiate the glory of the figures painted on them – whether Jesus, the Virgin Mary or one of the saints. They are 'peep-holes into eternity' bringing worshippers into contact with the beauties of the world beyond this one.

A-Z **In the Glossary**

Altar ~ Bible ~ Gospels ~ Holy Communion ~ Holy Liturgy ~ Holy Spirit ~ Icon ~ Iconostasis ~ Last Supper ~ Lord's Prayer ~ Mass ~ Nicene Creed ~ Orthodox Church ~ Priest ~ Royal Doors ~ Saint ~ Virgin Mary

[B] Why does the priest prepare the elements of bread and wine out of the people's sight behind the iconostasis?

Read Luke 22.7-13; 1 Corinthians 11.17-34

5:8 | The Breaking of Bread

Nonconformists try to keep their worship as close to the Bible as possible. This is why they have two favourite terms for Holy Communion:

1] **'THE BREAKING OF BREAD'** which is a direct description taken from the New Testament of the meal that the early Christians shared with each other [see box 1].

2] **'THE LORD'S SUPPER'** which was the favourite description of St Paul for the meal [see box 2].

The early Christians often met together for an ordinary meal. Quite apart from being an act of worship in itself this meal also served the practical purpose of feeding those who were poor and needy in the church community. The meal was also a symbolic act since, by bringing together the poor and the wealthy in the Christian community, it was a practical demonstration of their unity and fellowship with each other – and with Christ.

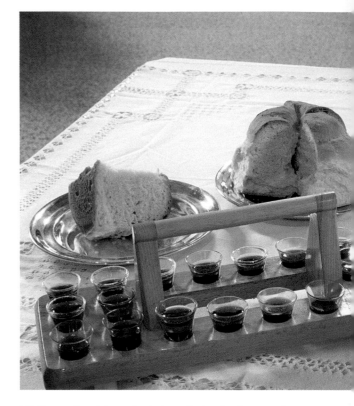

[A] Nonconformists prefer to have their wine in separate glasses. Can you think of any symbolic reason for this?

Breaking bread

In most Nonconformist churches the Breaking of Bread is celebrated twice a month – after the morning and evening services. In the service:

1] The people begin by confessing their sins before listening to a passage read from the Bible. This passage might describe the last meal that Jesus ate with his disciples [Luke 22.7-13] or Paul's description of the Eucharist [1 Corinthians 11.17-34]. The minister then spends a short time explaining the meaning of the passage and the importance of everyone sharing communion together before a collection is taken up for the needy in the local Christian community.

2] The cloth covering the bread and wine on the communion table is removed. There is no altar in a Nonconformist church. The wine is usually in separate glasses which are slotted into a double-tiered tray. The bread is cut up into small squares. The bread and wine are consecrated to God as the minister, or service leader, reads the words spoken by Jesus at the Last Supper [see box 3].

c. In Methodist churches the people come forward and kneel at the rail around the communion table to receive the bread and wine. In other Nonconformist churches, however, the church

BOX 1

ACTS 20.7

On the first day of the week [Sunday] we came together to break bread.

BOX 2

1.Corinthians 11.33

So, then, my brothers and sisters, when you gather together to eat the Lord's Supper, wait for one another.

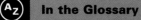 **In the Glossary**

Altar ~ Bible ~ Breaking of Bread ~ Disciple ~ Eucharist ~ Holy Communion ~ Last Supper ~ Lord's Supper ~ Mass ~ Minister ~ New Testament ~ Nonconformist ~ Paul ~ Protestant ~ Reformation ~ Transubstantiation

In the early Church there was a mixture of wealthy and poor members. Why do you think it was important for them to demonstrate that they were united? How do you think that this could be demonstrated in the Church today?

1 a. Describe a Breaking of Bread service as it is celebrated in a Nonconformist church.
b. By what other name may this service also be known?
c. On which event in the Bible is this service based?

2 Describe THREE important pieces of symbolism that are embedded in a Nonconformist Breaking of Bread service.

3 Explain why, in a Nonconformist Breaking of Bread service:
a. The people eat the bread when they receive it.
b. The people wait until everyone has been served with the wine before drinking it.

leaders [called elders or deacons] take the elements to the people in their seats. When the bread is given to them they eat it immediately to symbolise the Protestant belief that salvation is an individual, personal matter between the person and God. When the glass of wine, though, is brought the people hold it until everyone else has been served before drinking together. This symbolises an equally important Protestant belief that the Church to which all true believers belong is one, united in fellowship with Christ.

the bread and wine are pointers to much more important spiritual realities. In taking, and consuming, the bread and wine each person is stimulated to think about the death and resurrection of Jesus. That is why the minister tells everyone, as they take the bread and wine, to: 'Feed on him [Jesus Christ] in your hearts by faith.'

[B] A minister leads the congregation in a Breaking of Bread service. What do you think members of the congregation will get from the service?

The meaning

Protestants do not believe that the bread and wine change during the Breaking of Bread – as the Catholics do in their Mass. During the Protestant Reformation in the 16th century this Catholic belief, transubstantiation, was emphatically rejected and it was this, more than anything else, that led to the formation of separate Protestant Churches. For those taking part in the Breaking of Bread service

BOX 3

MARK 14.22-24

While they were eating, Jesus took a piece of bread, gave a prayer of thanks, broke it, and gave it to his disciples, 'Take it,' he said, 'this is my body.' Then he took a cup, gave thanks to God, and handed it to them; and they all drank from it. Jesus said, 'This is my blood which is poured out for many, my blood which seals God's covenant.'

6:1 | Infant Baptism

Infant baptism refers to the service in many churches when babies are baptised with water. There is no clear reference in the New Testament to infant baptism. It was not until the 4th century that Christian families began to have their children baptised. This happened because the belief grew up that unbaptised babies, many of whom died in infancy, would not go to heaven. Today infant baptism is an important sacrament in the Anglican, Roman Catholic and Orthodox Churches.

The font

The ceremony usually takes place within a few months of birth and is the means by which a baby becomes a member of the Church family. In most churches the font, the receptacle in which the water is placed for baptism, stands just inside the door. This is to symbolise the traditional belief that infant baptism is the door through which a person passes into full membership of the Church. Sometimes, though, the font used is portable and placed in the middle of the congregation for the service. This shows that the church family is taking responsibility for the spiritual growth of the child in the years ahead.

Infant baptism

There are some variations between the different Churches in the way that the ceremony is carried out:

1] Anglican and Roman Catholic Churches In these Churches a child is presented for baptism by its parents and godparents. The godparents accept the responsibility of watching over the spiritual upbringing of the child. In the Catholic Church at least one of the godparents must be a committed Roman Catholic. Both parents and godparents are asked to affirm their own religious faith by answering several

[A] What do you think is the main reason why most parents bring their baby to be baptised?

BOX 1

THE BOOK OF COMMON PRAYER

Baptism is not only a sign of profession, and mark of difference, whereby Christian men [and women] are discerned from others that be not christened, but it is also a sign of Regeneration or New Birth... The Baptism of young Children is in any wise to be retained in the Church.

Talk it over

Recently several vicars have refused to baptise babies because their parents do not have a clear Christian commitment or do not go to church. Do you think this is a reasonable attitude for them to take?

[B] What role are godparents expected to play in the life of a child?

questions – about their belief in God the Father, Jesus and the Holy Spirit. In a Catholic service they are also asked whether they believe in the forgiveness of sins, in the resurrection of the body and in life everlasting.

The child is then baptised with water being poured over its head three times 'in the name of the Father, and of the Son and of the Holy Spirit' whilst the priest makes the sign of the cross on its forehead. After the baby has been baptised the parents are often handed a lighted candle to symbolise the fact that the child has moved from darkness to light. The whole congregation tells the child: 'We welcome you into the Lord's family. We are members together of the body of Christ; we are children of the same Heavenly Father; we are inheritors together of the kingdom of God.'

Parents who bring their child for baptism believe that this ceremony marks the spiritual rebirth of the child as others renounce evil and repent on its behalf. The child can return much later at confirmation [see 6.2] to make the same vows for himself or herself.

2] Orthodox Church Admission into membership of the Orthodox Church is by baptism followed, in the same service, by chrismation [confirmation]. During the service of baptism evil spirits are symbolically driven out and the oil and the water used in the service are blessed. After doing this the priest anoints the baby with the 'oil of gladness'. The baby is undressed, placed in the font facing east – the direction of the rising sun and a symbol of new life – and immersed totally beneath the water.

The ceremony of chrismation follows immediately after baptism. For this the child is anointed all over with oil. Chrism is a mixture of olive oil and balsam, together with other ingredients, that is used in anointing in baptism, confirmation and ordination. Finally the baby is dressed in a new white robe to symbolise the eternal life which has been given to the child through baptism.

In the Glossary

Anglican Church ~ Baptism ~ Chrismation ~ Confirmation ~ Font ~ Holy Spirit ~ Infant Baptism ~ New Testament ~ Ordination ~ Orthodox Church ~ Priest ~ Roman Catholic Church ~ Sacrament

Work to do

1 Describe what happens at an infant baptism service.

2 'All Christian parents should have their children baptised.' Do you agree with this point of view?

3 Write a description of the part that infant baptism plays in the life of many churches.

4 Why is the font an important symbol in many churches?

5 Why do some Christians think that infant baptism is important?

6 a. Describe THREE pieces of symbolism in the infant baptism service.
b. What do these pieces of symbolism mean?

BOX 2

THE ALTERNATIVE SERVICE BOOK

Children who are too young to profess the faith are baptised on the understanding that they are brought up as Christians within the family of the Church.

6:2 Confirmation

KEY QUESTION

WHY IS CONFIRMATION AN IMPORTANT SERVICE IN MANY CHURCHES AND WHAT DOES IT MEAN?

During the time of the early Christian Church a bishop baptised all new Christian converts in his diocese and 'laid his hands' on them. When infant baptism became the usual practice of the Church the 'laying-on-of-hands' became the service of confirmation. In the Roman Catholic Church infant baptism and confirmation were separated but the Orthodox Church retained the traditional practice of celebrating the two in the same service.

Preparation for confirmation

In the Roman Catholic Church confirmation, together with the taking of the first communion, kick-starts the spiritual life which began at baptism. At baptism a child receives the Holy Spirit but the Spirit lies dormant in that person until it is awakened at confirmation. In the Catholic tradition a person can be confirmed as early as six years old but in the Anglican Church it does not happen until their teenage years. Adult converts in both Churches can be baptised and confirmed in the same service.

Confirmation classes are held before the service to prepare those who are taking part. During these classes the meaning of the sacrament is discussed. Some time is spent studying the life of Jesus and the apostles to see how the Holy Spirit played an important part in their lives. Sometimes a special time of prayer, or going away on a retreat, plays a part in the preparation. Those preparing in a Roman Catholic church receive the sacrament of reconciliation [see 5.3] before they are confirmed. Everyone is encouraged to form the habit of

[A] What do you think confirmation means for those being confirmed?

regularly reading their Bible and praying in the hope that this will continue as a spiritual discipline after they have been confirmed.

The Confirmation Service

During the Confirmation Service the same questions asked of parents and godparents at baptism [see 6.1] are repeated. This time, though, the person is old enough to answer the questions for themselves to show that they are now taking responsibility for their own spiritual welfare. When the questions have been answered the bishop lays his hands on the head of each candidate. This practice goes back to the early Church as an indication now, as it was then, that the Holy Spirit has been given to the person. Two further features of the service in a Roman Catholic

BOX 1

ACTS 13 2-3

While they were worshipping the Lord and fasting, the Holy Spirit said, 'Set apart for me Barnabas and Saul for the work to which I have called them.' So after they had fasted and prayed, they placed their hands on them, and sent them off.

BOX 2

CONFIRMATION SERVICE ROMAN CATHOLIC

God our Father, you sent the Holy Spirit upon the apostles, and through them and their successors you give the Spirit to your people. May his work begun at Pentecost continue to grow in the hearts of all who believe.

Talk it over

In the Glossary

If confirmation is a time for
committing oneself to the Christian
way of life when do you think is the
best time for this to take place?

Anglican Church ~ Apostle ~ Baptism ~ Bible
~ Bishop ~ Chrismation ~ Confirmation ~
Holy Spirit ~ Methodist Church ~ Orthodox
Church ~ Reconciliation ~ Roman Catholic
Church ~ Sacrament

church are worth noting:

1] The candidates are anointed with oil [chrism].
In Biblical times oil was rubbed into wounds as a
healing agent. Here it is the healing of the soul,
rather than the body, which is symbolised by the oil.

2] The bishop lightly slaps the face of each person
with two fingers. This symbolic gesture highlights
the suffering and contempt that each new
Christian might have to face now that an open
commitment to Christ has been made.

The service of confirmation represents a new
beginning – with all the peace of mind that comes
from having one's sins forgiven.

The Methodist Church

There is a confirmation service in the Methodist
Church although this Church does not have
bishops to conduct it. In the Methodist Church a
person who has already been baptised becomes a
church member through confirmation when the
hands of the minister are placed on his or her
head. Each succeeding year, following this,
Methodists sign a ticket of membership [see box 3]
which commits them to carry out several
responsibilities in the church and in the outside
world. This covenant [agreement] is renewed at the
annual covenant service which takes place on the
first Sunday of the year in every Methodist church.

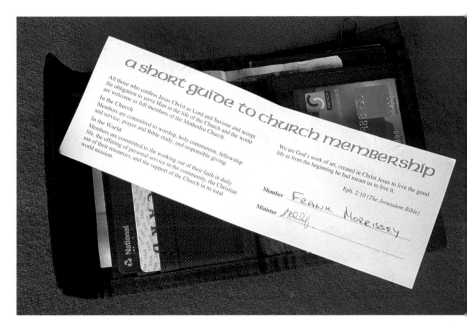

BOX 3

THE METHODIST COVENANT

*All those who confess Jesus Christ as
Lord and Saviour and accept the
obligation to serve him in the life of the
Church and the world are welcome as full
members of the Methodist Church.
In the Church: Members are committed
to worship, Holy Communion, fellowship
and service, prayer and Bible study,
and responsible giving.
In the world: Members are committed to the
working out of their faith in daily life, the
offering of personal service in the community,
the Christian use of resources, and the support
of the Church in its total world mission.*

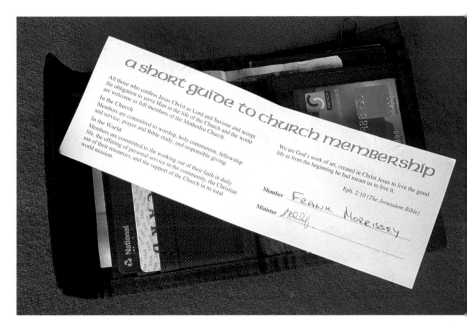

Work to do

1 Describe what happens and what is said
in the sacrament of confirmation.

2 Describe TWO pieces of symbolism
which take place in a confirmation
service and explain what they mean.

3 The Church teaches that people receive
the blessing of the Holy Spirit when
they are confirmed. What kind of difference
do you think this might make to their lives?

4 a. Why do many Christians regard
confirmation as an important part of
their Christian commitment?
b. Why do people attend confirmation
classes and what happens in them?

5 Describe THREE features of
confirmation.

[B] What level of
commitment is being
demanded of those who
become members of
the Methodist Church?

Read Matthew 3.13-17; Acts 10.48; 18.8

6:3 Believer's Baptism

KEY QUESTION

WHY DO SOME CHURCHES INSIST ON ONLY BAPTISING BELIEVING ADULTS?

The Baptist Church, as well as a few other Nonconformist Churches, insist that the only possible kind of baptism is that involving believing adults. This, they argue, is the only form of baptism to be found in the New Testament. To support their argument they point out that:

1] Jesus himself was baptised by John the Baptist in the River Jordan [A] when he was thirty years old [*Matthew 3.13-17*]. John was baptising people who repented [were sorry] for their sins but, as Jesus was sinless, this could not explain his wish to be baptised. It seems that he wanted to identify himself with those people who knew that they were sinners and needed God's forgiveness even if he didn't.

2] Peter, on the Day of Pentecost [*see 1.2*], told his converts to '…turn away from your sins and be baptised in the name of Jesus Christ, so that your sins will be forgiven and you will receive God's gift, the Holy Spirit.' [*Acts 2.38*]. From that time onwards in the early Church these four elements – repentance, baptism, forgiveness and receiving the Holy Spirit – were often linked. Together they formed the basis of the message that the early Christians preached.

3] Paul used the symbolism of baptism to explain what happened in the Christian life [see box 2]. Going down into the waters represents a death to the old life whilst leaving the waters after baptism speaks of life beyond death. This symbolism is only accurate if applied to believer's baptism.

BOX 1

MARK 1.9-11

Not long afterwards Jesus came from Nazareth in the province of Galilee and was baptised by John in the Jordan. As soon as Jesus came up out of the water, he saw heaven opening and the Spirit coming down on him like a dove. And a voice came from heaven: 'You are my own dear Son. I am pleased with you.'

[A] Why do you think that the example of Jesus is so important to those people who are being baptised?

Believer's Baptism

In the early Church the baptism of believers was only performed at Easter or Whitsun but now it can be carried out at any time, in any suitable place. Some Christians travel to the River Jordan for it so that they can follow in the footsteps of Jesus whilst others are baptised in a nearby sea or local river. They want to use the opportunity of witnessing in the open-air to others of their faith in Jesus. The majority, though, are baptised in a special baptistry which is sunk into the floor at the front of a Baptist church.

Before a baptism takes place classes are held to explain the meaning and symbolism of the service. It is very important that everyone understands exactly what they are doing. During the service itself each person is given the opportunity to

Talk it over

Why do you think that some Christians feel very deeply that baptism should be confined to adult Christian believers?

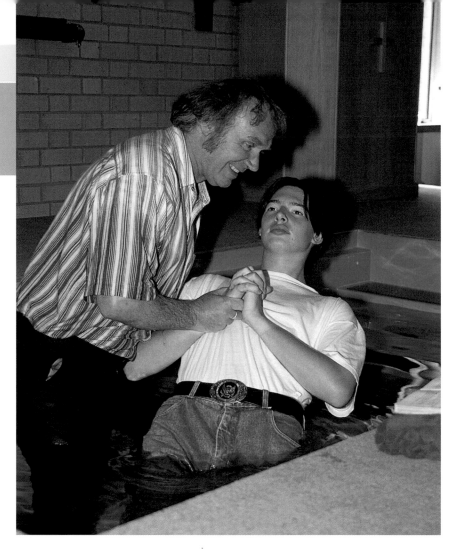

[B] What do you think is the most important part of the service of believer's baptism?

explain the reason why they are being baptised. They describe how they became a Christian and why they now want to follow the example of Jesus by being baptised. Then each person:

1] Goes down into the water where the minister of the church is waiting to receive them. By going down into the pool the person is showing to everyone their desire to leave their old sinful life and all that it represents behind them.

2] Is totally immersed beneath the waters of the pool [B]. Although this only lasts for a brief moment it is a very important part of the service. Just as Jesus was buried in the tomb after being crucified so the person is now being spiritually 'buried' with Christ. This 'dying with Christ' is at the heart of Believer's Baptism.

3] Comes up out of the water and leaves the pool by a different set of steps. This shows that the person has already begun to share the 'resurrection life' of Jesus. When Jesus rose from the dead he did not have his old life and body. Everything was different. In the same way, after baptism, the person is expected to live a new life – the Christian life. They now share in the eternal life which Jesus shares with his Father in heaven and with the Holy Spirit.

It is important to realise that nothing actually happens to a person through Believer's Baptism. This baptism which has taken place is merely a 'picture' of changes that have taken place, and continue to take place, in the life of the Christian.

BOX 2

ROMANS 6.4

By our baptism, then, we were buried with him and shared his death, in order that, just as Christ was raised from death by the glorious power of the Father, so also we might live a new life.

 In the Glossary

Baptism ~ Baptist Church ~ Believer's Baptism ~ Day of Pentecost ~ Easter Day ~ Holy Spirit ~ John the Baptist ~ Minister ~ New Testament ~ Nonconformist Church ~ Paul ~ Peter ~ Whitsun

▶ **Work to do**

1 Why do Baptists believe that only adults, and not children, should be baptised?

2 Describe what happens at a Believer's Baptism service.

3 Describe and explain TWO important pieces of symbolism found in a Believer's Baptism.

4 Explain the symbolic importance of the following in the service of Believer's Baptism:
a. The waters of baptism.
b. The lowering of the body into the water.
c. The act of baptism.
d. The leaving of the water.

5 Imagine that you are a Baptist who has just been baptised and you are anxious to explain to two of your friends what has happened - and what it means. What would you say to them?

Read Matthew 19.4-6

6:4 Marriage

WHAT HAPPENS DURING A CHRISTIAN WEDDING CEREMONY?

[A] Why do you think that almost half of the couples marrying still choose to do so in a church?

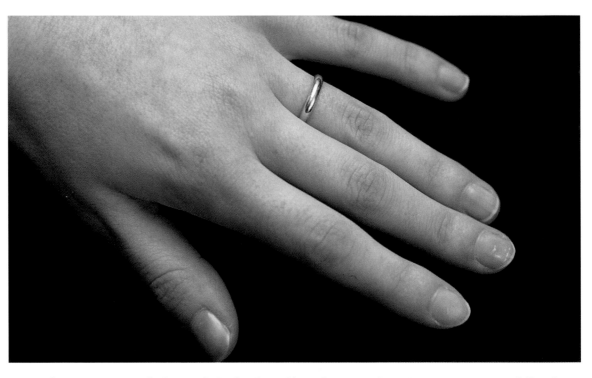

In the Roman Catholic and Orthodox Churches marriage is a sacrament. Whilst the other Churches do not see it in quite the same way it is, in all denominations, a binding agreement made between two people who love each other in the sight of God. This unending love is described by Paul as a reflection of the love that Jesus has for his 'bride', the Church [box 1].

BOX 1

EPHESIANS 5.31-33

As the Scripture says: 'For this reason a man will leave his father and mother and unite with his wife, and the two will become one.' There is a deep secret truth in this scripture, which I understand as applying to Christ and his Church. But it also applies to you: every husband must love his wife as himself, and every wife must respect her husband.

The reasons for marriage

In the modern Anglican wedding service the priest provides the couple with three Christian reasons for marriage:

a. *Reason 1* So that two people can love and care for each other. Marriage provides the secure and stable relationship in which this can best take place. They are to live together faithfully through need and plenty, in sorrow and in joy.

b. *Reason 2* To provide the most secure environment in which sexual intercourse can take place. They are to know each other with

Work to do

1 a. What are the vows in a wedding service?
b. What do the man and the woman promise each other?

2 What is the symbolic meaning of the ring in the wedding service?

3 Describe a Christian wedding service.

4 If a couple take the marriage ceremony seriously how do you think it might influence their married lives together?

joy and tenderness so that their sexual union may strengthen the bonding of their hearts and souls.

c. *Reason 3* To provide a loving and stable environment into which children can be born and brought up. They must accept the gift of children with thankfulness to God and bring them up as Christians.

The marriage ceremony

In the modern Anglican service the emphasis is very much upon the love between the two people. The prayer with which the service begins makes this clear: 'God our Father, you have taught us through your Son that love is the fulfiling of the law. Grant to your servants that, loving one another, they may continue in your love until their lives' end; through Jesus Christ our Lord. Amen.'

During the service the couple express this love by making vows to each other [see box 2]. These vows are the part of the wedding service which is required by law. The man then places a ring on the third finger of the bride's left hand [they may exchange rings instead] and offers it as a symbol of their commitment to each other [A]. In all Churches the ring, a perfect and unbroken circle, is taken as a symbol of that love which, if genuine, will last for ever. The priest pronounces them husband and wife with the words: 'That which God has joined together, let no man divide.'

Two important variations should be noted:
1] When a marriage takes place between two Roman Catholics the wedding service is ended with the celebration of a Nuptual Mass. The Mass celebrated in a wedding is unique amongst Catholic sacraments. All of the other sacraments are bestowed by the priest on the celebrants but in the Nuptual Mass the husband and wife give the elements of bread and wine to each other. By so doing the couple are expressing their love for each other and their love for God.

2] In the Greek Orthodox wedding service a 'crowning' takes place. The priest crowns the couple with 'wreaths' indicating that they will become king and queen over their own small kingdom - the house that they will be setting up together. The crowns are made of leaves and flowers of silver and gold. To symbolise this unity the couple share a glass of wine with each other and walk three times, hand in hand, around a table in the middle of the church.

A Quaker wedding

In a Quaker meeting house the wedding starts with silent prayer and reflection. After a few minutes the couple stand and make their vows to each other. Holding each other's hand they say: 'Friends, I take this Friend [name] to be my wife/husband, promising through divine assistance, to be unto him/her a loving wife/husband, so long as we both on earth shall live.' The couple sign the register, followed by the other people in the meeting. The meeting then continues silently.

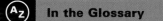

In the Glossary

Anglican Church ~ Nuptual Mass ~ Orthodox Church ~ Paul ~ Priest ~ Quaker ~ Roman Catholic Church ~ Sacrament

---

BOX 2

THE WEDDING VOWS

I, N, take you, N, to be my wife [husband], to have and to hold, from this day forward; For better, for worse, for richer, for poorer, in sickness and in health, to love and to cherish, till death us do part, according to God's holy law, and this is my solemn vow.

BOX 3

WITH THE GIVING OF THE RING

I give you this ring as a sign of our marriage. With my body I honour you, all that I am I give to you, and all that I have I share with you, within the love of God the Father, the Son and the Holy Spirit.

6:5 | Funerals

Talk it over

The Christian funeral services are based on the belief that the soul survives death. Is this a belief that you share?

The clear ideas which Christians hold about life after death *[see 2.10]* are reflected in the funeral services of the different denominations. Above all, each service reflects the belief that death is not the end and that the soul lives on after the body dies. At the end of time, when Christ returns to the earth, each person will be resurrected to share in his victory over death. Death will then be finally abolished.

KEY QUESTION

WHAT BELIEFS ABOUT LIFE AFTER DEATH ARE REFLECTED IN A CHRISTIAN FUNERAL SERVICE?

BOX 1

GENESIS 3.19

By the sweat of your brow you will eat your food until you return to the ground, since from it you were taken; for dust you are and to dust you will return.

Orthodox funerals

In the Orthodox Church there is no difference between those who are alive and those who have died. This is what Orthodox believers mean by the 'Communion of the Saints'. Just as we pray for those who are alive so we must pray for the dead. These prayers begin as soon as a person has died. The body is washed, dressed in new clothes and placed in an open coffin. An icon is put in the hand of the corpse and a strip of material containing other icons stretched across the forehead. The body is then covered with a linen cloth to symbolise the protection that Christ offers everyone – alive and dead – who believes.

[A] How do you know that this coffin is not in an Orthodox church?

Since death is always a tragedy in the Orthodox Church so it must bring grief and a great sense of loss. Even here, though, there is real hope for the Christian believer. In the Orthodox funeral service the burning candles express the hope of eternal life. Everyone is encouraged to look beyond the present to a future time when Jesus will return to the earth – and all the dead will be brought back to life.

Protestant and Catholic funerals

The same strong belief that death is not the end is stressed in funerals held in Protestant and Roman Catholic churches:

1] A Protestant funeral When a person has died their soul is committed to the safe keeping of God's care and protection. This is done first of all in a short service which has hymns, prayers, a Bible reading and an eulogy [a song of praise] about the dead person. Everything in the service underlines the Protestant belief that once a person dies their soul goes straight to be with God in heaven. It also looks forward to the end of time when the dead will be raised and Christ's kingdom will be set up on earth.

BOX 2

THE KONTAKION - A GREEK ORTHODOX FUNERAL PRAYER

Give rest, O Christ, to all thy servants with thy saints. Where sorrow and pain are no more, neither sighing but life everlasting. Thou only art immortal, the creator and maker of man, and we are mortal born of earth, and unto earth we will return, all we go down to the dust.

Work to do

1 A Christian funeral reflects Christian beliefs about life after death. How would you sum those beliefs up?

2 'A Christian funeral should be a joyful as well as a sad occasion.' What is said at a Christian funeral to offer encouragement and hope? Look at the extracts in boxes 2 and 3.

3 Describe a Christian funeral and explain how it reflects one main Christian belief.

4 Read box 1. How would you sum up the belief about life after death which is expressed here?

5 Read the Kontakion in box 2.
a. In which Church is this used as a funeral prayer?
b. How would you sum up the belief about life after death which is expressed in this prayer?

The Christian funeral service is similar whether the person is being buried or cremated. In the case of someone being buried a short 'committal' takes place at the graveside during which the body of the dead person is committed to the safe keeping of God. Words are read from the book of Genesis [box 1] reminding everyone that they were formed originally from dust and it is to dust that they return at the end of their earthly life.

2] A Catholic funeral In the Roman Catholic community the coffin is taken to the church on the night before the funeral [A]. This allows time for prayers to be said for the soul of the deceased. This is important because, Catholics believe, the soul of each person spends time in 'purgatory' – a place between heaven and hell – before their final destiny is decided by God. The prayers which people offer on earth can affect the length of time that a soul spends in purgatory.

The priest dresses in white for the service since this is the colour traditionally associated with life after death and the resurrection of the body. The service takes the form of a Requiem Mass during which the prayer, 'Eternal rest grant unto them, O Lord, and let light perpetual rest on them' is offered up. As the coffin is lowered into the grave the priest says the words: "Father, into your hands we commend our brother [sister]. We are confident that with all who have died in Christ he/she will be raised to life on the last day and live with Christ forever.'

BOX 3

FUNERAL PRAYER USED BY THE UNITED REFORMED CHURCH

For as much as it has pleased Almighty God of His great mercy to take unto himself the soul of our dear brother/sister departed, we therefore commit his/her body to the ground; earth to earth, ashes to ashes, dust to dust; in sure and certain hope of the resurrection to everlasting life through our Lord Jesus Christ.

[B] What might a Christian say to this person to offer them some hope?

97

7:1 | Monastic Life

[A] What is the link between work and prayer in the life of a monk?

Some of the early Christians wanted to dedicate themselves totally to God. Following the example of Jesus they made their way into the desert to live a life dedicated to prayer and meditation. St Anthony of Egypt was the first but he was soon followed by many others. There were two reasons why they believed the desert was a spiritually important location:

1] As there were no material comforts in the desert, people were free to live a life of self-denial.
2] Evil spirits were believed to make their home in the desert. Any person who lived there placed themselves in the front-line of the battle between good and evil in the world.

To begin with these people lived solitary lives as hermits but they soon formed communities, known as monasteries. One of the earliest monasteries was on Mount Athos in Greece and this is still populated by many Greek Orthodox monks.

The three vows

St Benedict [480-547] was the most influential figure in the history of monasticism because he laid down the 'Rule' by which monasteries and convents still organise their communal life today. The Rule stipulates that all monks and nuns should live:

> **BOX 1**
>
> **MARK 10.21**
>
> *Go, sell everything you have and give to the poor, and you will have treasure in heaven. Then come, follow me.*

1] **A life of total poverty** When the rich young man came to Jesus he was told to go away and sell all that he had if he wanted to be a disciple [box 1]. Those entering a Religious Order must transfer all the property and wealth they have to the institution. As some Religious Orders dedicate themselves to working amongst the poor it would be unthinkable for them not to share the poverty of those around them.

2] **A celibate life** Those in a Religious Order do not enter into any kind of sexual or emotional relationship since this would make it impossible for them to devote themselves single-mindedly to God's work. Only those totally committed can devote themselves to the task of building up God's kingdom on earth. Marriage interferes with such commitment. Monks and nuns speak of themselves instead as being 'married' to God.

> **BOX 2**
>
> **RULE OF ST BENEDICT**
>
> *Idleness is the enemy of the soul. And, therefore, at fixed times, the brothers ought to be occupied in manual labour; and again, at fixed times, in sacred reading.*

1 Members of Religious Orders take the three vows of poverty, chastity and obedience.
a. Explain what each of these vows means.
b. Show how they help members of the Religious Orders to live their lives.

2 a. What are apostolic and contemplative Religious Orders?
b. What is the main difference between them?

3] A life of obedience Those who enter a monastery or a convent are expected to live in total obedience to the will of the community - as it is expressed through the Abbot or the Mother Superior. These leaders are chosen by the monks and nuns themselves because of the holiness of their lives.

The Rule emphasises the close link between community prayer, work and relaxation in the monastic life. Traditionally prayers have been offered seven times a day in religious communities but modern communities, whilst still underlining the importance of prayer, have reduced the number of times that the monks or nuns meet together to pray.

Contemplative Orders

Many of the Religious Orders are called 'apostolic'. Although their communal way of life means that they have withdrawn from the world in a real sense they still work outside the monastery or convent. Many monks and nuns work as teachers, nurses, or parish workers. Any money they earn goes directly to the monastery or convent. As they have taken the vow of celibacy so they still continue to live their lives in the community and prayer still plays a very important part in this.

Some Religious Orders, however, follow a contemplative approach to life. These monks and nuns withdraw as much as they can from contact with the outside world and rarely leave their monastery or convent. Contemplatives place a high degree of importance on silence within the community. Meals, for instance, are often taken in silence or with someone reading to them from a holy book. Whilst some time is given over to work within the community much time is spent in prayer, reading and studying.

In the Glossary

Celibacy ~ Convent ~ Monastery ~ Monk ~ Nun

BOX 3

RULE OF ST FRANCIS

This is the Rule and way of life of the brothers minor; to observe the holy Gospel of our Lord Jesus Christ, living in obedience, without personal possessions, and in chastity.

[B] What does it mean when a nun speaks of being 'married' to God?

7:2 | Iona and Taize

Whilst the old monastic traditions and Orders still survive today they have failed to capture the imagination of young people. Instead, the young have turned in increasing numbers to such communities as those established at Iona, in Scotland, and at Taizé, in France. These two communities embrace many of the old monastic ideals but also take on board modern Christian concerns as well.

Iona

Iona is an island almost a mile off the Scottish coast. St Columba arrived on the island with some monks to begin the task of spreading the Christian message in the north of England and Scotland in 563 CE. Much has been written about Columba's attractive personality; his skill as a bard and scribe; his visions and prophecies and his miraculous powers such as he showed when he expelled a water monster from Loch Ness by making the sign of the cross over the water. Although the monastery he built on Iona has long since disappeared it remained a holy place to many and pilgrims found their way there for centuries.

During the 1930s its popularity as a destination

[A] How do you think the location of Iona contributes to its spiritual importance?

Work to do

1 a. What is the dominant theme of the Taizé community?
b. How did this theme spring out of the time when the Taize community was born?

2 Look at the quote in box 1 carefully:
a. What do you think the Rule means by 'That Christ may grow in me...?
b. Why do you think it is essential for a person living in a community to be aware of his own weaknesses?
c. Why do you think someone in a community needs to be aware of the weaknesses of others?
d. What do you think is meant by: 'For them I will become all things to all, and even give my life, for Christ's sake and the Gospel's'?

3 Compare the covenant into which members of the Iona community enter with the traditional Rule of St Benedict. Which do you think is more in tune with life today?

for pilgrims increased and in 1938 the Rev George MacLeod rebuilt the monastery using unemployed people from the poor areas of Glasgow. Iona soon became popular with visitors who could talk and pray in a place of immense tranquillity and peace. Gradually, a new lifestyle associated with Iona began to emerge. The monastery there does not have any permanent monks or nuns but a group of people who pledge themselves to:

1] Spend one week a year on the island taking part in physical and spiritual activities with other members of the community.

2] Spend time each day at home reading the Bible and praying.

3] Give 10% of their money to the Church and to work within their own community for peace, reconciliation and justice.

4] Follow a vegetarian life-style based on a respect for all of God's creatures - animal and human.

Taizé

Taizé is an international place of pilgrimage in south-east France. It offers spiritual refreshment to a wide cross-section of people, mostly young, who are drawn from all Protestant and Roman Catholic denominations. Since 1949 people have travelled to Taizé to join with the monastic community there in its worship - a worship which places reconciliation between all people and simplicity of worship at the centre of its life.

The Taizé community began in 1940 when Roger Schutz, now known as Brother Roger and the community's leader, began to live on his own as a monk. Soon many refugees who were fleeing from the Nazis joined him. The war forced him to leave the area but he returned in 1946. He took in German prisoners of war and this made him very unpopular with some people in the area but he realised the importance of reconciliation in the world. Today some eighty monks live in the community with many others scattered throughout the world in similar communities. At Taizé and elsewhere they see themselves as 'signs of the presence of Christ among men and women and the bearers of God's joy...'

In 1962 a group of German Christians built the Church of Reconciliation at Taizé and this is the centre of the community's worship. The worship is built around chants which are sung in Latin, English, French and German. Candles burn brightly during services and icons are found everywhere to help people to centre their thoughts and worship. Visitors are invited to spend a week worshipping with the monks and then to spend, if they wish, a further week in a silent retreat.

BOX 1
PART OF THE RULE OF TAIZE
That Christ may grow in me, I must know my own weakness and that of my brothers. For them I will become all things to all, and even give my life, for Christ's sake and the Gospel's.

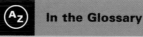 **In the Glossary**

Bible ~ Icon ~ Monastery ~ Monk ~ Nun ~ Protestant ~ Roman Catholic Church

7:3 Pilgrimages

KEY QUESTION

WHY ARE
PILGRIMAGES
AN IMPORTANT
PART OF THE
CHRISTIAN
EXPERIENCE
FOR SOME
CHRISTIANS?

A pilgrimage is a spiritual journey to a holy place and those who undertake one are called pilgrims. Pilgrims travel to special holy places because they believe that this will help to draw them closer to God. Undertaking a pilgrimage is an important part of most religions but it does not play a central role in Christianity. Even so, there are thousands of Christian pilgrims who set off each year in search of a closer relationship with God.

Why go on a pilgrimage?

In the main it has been Roman Catholics who have undergone pilgrimages whilst Protestants have, over the centuries, shown little interest in the idea. There are several reasons for undertaking a pilgrimage:

1] To thank God for a blessing. Some pilgrims, seeking God's help or healing, have made a promise that they will undertake a pilgrimage if their prayer is answered.

2] To visit the places that are important, and holy, to faith. For many pilgrims, it is an important part of their Christian faith that they visit the land in which Jesus lived, taught and died – Palestine. More about this in 7.4 but thousands of Christians visit the Holy Land each year especially during the festivals of Christmas and Easter. The birthplace of Jesus [Bethlehem] and the place where he died [Jerusalem] draw most pilgrims but people also want to see the other places mentioned in the Gospels. In experiencing some of the atmosphere there they hope to gain a deeper knowledge of the Gospels and the Jesus of whom they speak.

3] To visit places where, it is believed, the Virgin Mary has appeared to people in the past. Lourdes and Walsingham [see 7.5], for instance, have both become important pilgrim destinations because of appearances of the Virgin. The same is true also of Knock, in Ireland, and Fatima, in Portugal.

4] To receive God's forgiveness for sins that have been committed. This was more true in the past than it is today. During the Middle Ages, for

▶ Work to do

1 How and why might the life of a Christian pilgrim be changed by going on a pilgrimage?

2 'Pilgrimage is not a very important activity for Christians.' Do you agree with this assessment. Give your reasons for reaching your conclusion.

3 a. Give THREE reasons why a person might choose to go on a pilgrimage today.
b. Do you find it surprising that people are still choosing to make these holy journeys at the start of the 21st century?

4 Pilgrims believe that they benefit from taking a pilgrimage. In what ways do you think this might be true?

5 'People go on a pilgrimage just to get away from it all.' Do you think this is true or is there a more serious motive for most people?

BOX 1

CHAUCER. THE CANTERBURY TALES

Thanne longen folk to goon on pilgrimages.

In the Glossary

 Talk it over

Christmas ~ Easter Day ~ Gospel ~
Jerusalem ~ Lourdes ~ Protestant ~ Roman
Catholic Church ~ Virgin Mary ~ Walsingham

Do you think that miraculous healings and happenings can still take place? If so, do you think they can still be associated with established pilgrimage sites - or is that mere superstition?

example, Canterbury became a very popular destination for pilgrims. They believed that such a pilgrimage not only wiped away their sins but also created much merit in purgatory for relatives and friends who had died. It was to Canterbury that King Henry II travelled seeking forgiveness in 1170 after being implicated in the death of Thomas Becket, the Archbishop of Canterbury four years earlier.

5] To pay homage to an important saint. Santiago de Compostela, in Spain, has been an important pilgrimage destination since the 9th century CE since it is believed that the bones of St James, a disciple of Jesus, were buried there. The Roman Catholic Church has always placed a high degree of importance on 'relics', the remains of someone holy from the past.

Many people return home from pilgrimages disappointed. Although people have been visiting Lourdes since the 19th century only a small number of 'miracle cures', claimed to have happened there, have defied all medical explanation. Millions have sought God's help, or blessing, at Lourdes and, for them, nothing has happened.

Others, though, have assessed the importance of pilgrimages, and visits to holy places, differently. They look at the whole experience in terms of spiritual growth and point out the importance of the fellowship enjoyed by pilgrims along the route. It is part of their spiritual journey and they return with their faith renewed and refreshed.

[A] The shrine at Knock, in Ireland. Why is this pilgrimage site believed to be important?

BOX 3

LEO TOLSTOY

Of what avail is it to go across the sea to Christ if all the time I lose the Christ that is within me here?

BOX 2

SIR WALTER RALEIGH

*Give me my scallop-shell of quiet,
My staff of faith to walk upon,
My scrip of joy, immortal diet,
My bottle of salvation,
My gown of glory, hope's true gage,
And thus I'll take my pilgrimage.*

7:4 Walsingham and Lourdes

KEY QUESTION

WHY HAVE WALSINGHAM AND LOURDES BEEN RECOGNISED AS VERY IMPORTANT PLACES OF PILGRIMAGE?

There are many 'holy places' in Great Britain and across Europe and most of these are associated with appearances of the Virgin Mary. For this reason they are far more likely to appeal to Roman Catholic and Orthodox pilgrims than to Protestants. In this unit we will look at two of the most popular holy places – Walsingham in England and Lourdes in France.

1] WALSINGHAM The shrine of Our Lady at Walsingham is the most popular destination for pilgrims in Great Britain. It was there, in 1061, that the Virgin Mary appeared to the lady of the manor, Lady Richeld. She was told to build a replica of the house in Nazareth where the Angel Gabriel had first appeared to Mary to tell her that she was going to give birth to Jesus. Lady Richeld built a simple wooden structure and placed a statue of the Virgin Mary inside. Her son was away fighting in the Crusades at the time, and whilst in the Holy Land visited the home of Mary. When he returned home he turned the simple building built by his mother into a much more beautiful house. He also endowed an Augustinian monastery on the site.

Small pilgrim shrines were built along the road to Walsingham. The last of these, the Slipper Chapel, was just a mile away. It was there that pilgrims removed their shoes to walk the last part of the pilgrimage barefoot. Almost everything was destroyed during the Reformation but the Slipper Chapel survived and this was reopened by Roman Catholics in 1934. Today both Roman Catholic and Anglican pilgrims travel to separate shrines in the town. The Greek and Russian Orthodox Churches also have shrines there. The holy wells in the town, thought to have arisen as a result of Lady Richeld's vision, are believed to have healing powers.

2] LOURDES In 1858 Bernadette Soubirous, aged fourteen, the daughter of a poor French family, saw a vision of a young, unknown, woman at a cave by the river in Lourdes. This small village is in the Pyrenees mountains, in the south of France. Bernadette's mother beat her when she learned of

(?) Find out

Lourdes and Walsingham are important pilgrimage sites but there are many others. Santiago de Compostela in Spain, Fatima in Portugal and Knock in Ireland are three others. Find out as much as you can about ONE of these pilgrimage destinations and write up your notes on it in your folder.

1 What do many Christians believe happened at Walsingham, in Norfolk?

2 Describe how Walsingham became the place of Christian pilgrimage for thousands of people that it is today.

3 Walsingham is believed to be a holy place yet the Roman Catholics, the Anglicans, the Greek and the Russian Orthodox Churches all have their separate shrines in the town. Does that strike you as very odd? Explain your answer - whatever it is.

4 Why did Lourdes, in France, become a very popular destination for Christian pilgrims in the 19th century?

5 What needs to have happened before the Roman Catholic Church is willing to accept that a miracle has taken place at Lourdes?

the visions for telling lies but they continued. After sixteen visions Bernadette asked the young woman who she was. The answer was: 'I am the Immaculate Conception,' an answer which Bernadette did not understand so she asked her parish priest who told her that she was having visions of the Virgin Mary. The site was recognised by the Church as holy in 1862 and in 1866 Bernadette became a nun. Bernadette was canonised by the Roman Catholic Church after dying in a convent at the age of thirty-five.

Pilgrims to Lourdes soon began to report miraculous healings and the number of people visiting it increased rapidly. In 1872 a rally of 20,000 people was held at the shrine. In 1958, one hundred years after the original vision, over 6,000,000 visitors travelled to the town. Each year at least 2,000,000 people visit Lourdes seeking God's blessing and healing. Any claim to a miracle is looked at carefully by a medical commission. To count as a miracle it must meet three conditions:

a. The cure must be sudden.

b. The cure must be complete.

c. The cure must be permanent of a serious, organic and documented illness or disease.

In 1999 the 66th medical healing of a person at Lourdes was announced – a Frenchman cured of multiple sclerosis. Despite this, the authorities of the Roman Catholic Church insist that people visit Lourdes out of religious devotion to the Virgin Mary - rather than in search of a cure. Volunteers make their own pilgrimage to Lourdes to look after those who cannot look after themselves. There are several churches on the site where people can pray or visit the Stations of the Cross. Sometimes they join in one of the many processions which parade around the site praying and singing. There is a candle-lit procession which takes place each night after dark. As a result of these spiritual activities Lourdes retains its prayerful and quiet atmosphere despite the large number of pilgrims who visit it.

[A] Are you inclined to believe that miracles take place in pilgrimage centres like Lourdes - or not?

(A-Z) **In the Glossary**

Anglican Church ~ Anglo-Catholics ~ Monastery ~ Nun ~ Orthodox Church ~ Priest ~ Roman Catholic Church ~ Stations of the Cross ~ Virgin Mary

7:5 | The Holy Land and Rome

[A] Pilgrims walking up the Via Dolorosa. Why do you think that doing this is an intensely moving experience for many Christians?

Another group of holy places of pilgrimage in Christianity are those associated with the life of Jesus and the early Christian Church, especially the apostle Peter. This takes us to the Holy Land of Israel, for the first, and to the city of Rome, in Italy, for the second:

1] THE HOLY LAND For centuries pilgrims have travelled to Israel to see the places where Jesus lived, taught and died. There are many places in the Holy Land which draw pilgrims but they visit most of them out of interest rather than feeling that they are visiting a holy site. They may go to Capernaum, where Jesus preached in the synagogue, or Cana in Galilee where, according to John's Gospel, he performed his first miracle when he changed water into wine. They visit the River Jordan where Jesus was baptised by John the Baptist or drive along the road from Jerusalem to Jericho where Jesus set his most well-known parable - that of the Good Samaritan. Often they visit these places on organised parties with guides who read appropriate passages from the Bible to them. Many find that to be in the very place where miracles took place or parables were told makes the Gospels come alive to them.

Two sites in the Holy Land, though, have a deeper significance for serious Christian pilgrims because of their close links with Jesus:

a. Bethlehem - the birthplace of Jesus. The spot where the stable in which Mary gave birth to Jesus is thought to have stood is now covered by the Church of the Nativity. Along with other important sites in the Holy Land this church is shared by many Christian denominations. The Greek Orthodox, Serbian Orthodox, Egyptian Orthodox and Roman Catholic Churches all have their own altars in the church served by their own priests. Two other churches in Bethlehem stand on the exact location where the Angel Gabriel is believed to have appeared to Mary telling her that she was going to bear God's Son [an event known as the 'Annunciation']. Most pilgrims visit Bethlehem over the Christmas festival to take part in the celebrations associated with the birth of Jesus. In recent years, though, there has been much violence in and around the town and the number of pilgrims visiting it has fallen.

BOX 1

WALTER HILTON, 15th CENTURY

If thou covet to come to this blessed site of very peace and be a true pilgrim to Jerusalem, though it be so that I was never there, nevertheless as far forth as I can I shall set thee on the way thitherward.

Talk it over

What arguments do you think a Christian who has been to the Holy Land might put to a sceptical Christian about the value of making a pilgrimage there?

In the Glossary

Bible ~ Christmas ~ Easter Day ~ Good Friday ~ Gospel ~ Jerusalem ~ John the Baptist ~ Orthodox Church ~ Parable ~ Peter ~ Pope ~ Priest ~ Roman Catholic Church ~ Station of the Cross ~ Virgin Mary

BOX 2

WILLIAM BLAKE

I will not cease from mental fight Nor shall my Sword sleep in my hand Till we have built Jerusalem In England's green and pleasant land.

b. Jerusalem. In Jerusalem there are many places associated with the last few days in the life of Jesus and this makes the city the main pilgrim destination in the Holy Land. Pilgrims make their way up the Via Dolorosa [the Way of Sorrows] to walk in the footsteps of Jesus as he made his way from Pilate's Judgment-Hall to his place of execution. On the way pilgrims pass the fourteen Stations of the Cross where the Bible and Church tradition say that Jesus stopped or fell on the journey. The same Stations are marked in every Roman Catholic church so that 'pilgrims' at home can undertake a similar 'pilgrimage'. Pilgrims stop at each Station to pray, and meditate, for a moment. On Good Friday pilgrims make their way up the Via Dolorosa behind someone carrying a large wooden cross. Churches are now standing on the traditional location of Golgotha [the place of a skull] where Jesus died as well as on the site of the Garden Tomb in which his body was laid.

2] ROME The city of Rome, in Italy, is an important destination for Roman Catholic pilgrims because of its many associations with the early Christians and the birth of the Church. Deep beneath the city are the Catacombs where the early Christians hid themselves to escape from persecution by the Roman emperors. Rome is of particular importance to Roman Catholics because it is the city in which St Peter, the first Bishop of Rome and Pope, was buried. The Pope, the head of the Roman Catholic Church, has his seat of power in the Vatican and pilgrims attend the weekly audience that he holds there. They also flock to St Peter's Square in their thousands on Easter Day when the Pope addresses them in over forty different languages.

[B] The Garden Tomb. What is significant about this place for visitors to Jerusalem?

Work to do

1 What do you think a Christian might gain from making a pilgrimage to:
a. The Holy Land?
b. Rome?

2 How and why might the life of a Christian be changed by going on a pilgrimage?

3 Explain what a Christian pilgrim would find in:
a. Bethlehem.
b. Jerusalem.

4 Explain why any TWO places have become centres of Christian pilgrimage.

8:1   The Christian Year

[A] This photograph shows an advent wreath. Find out something about the symbolic meaning of this wreath.

The Christian Year is the regular pattern of festivals and celebrations on which most Christians base their church worship. Regularly during the year festivals are held to commemorate, and celebrate, important events in the life of Jesus and the early Church. The most important of these festivals are Christmas and Easter but Advent, Epiphany, Lent, Ascension Day and Whitsun also play their part in the liturgy of most Churches. The festivals are most faithfully celebrated in the Roman Catholic and Orthodox Churches although the latter celebrates most of them on different dates. These two Churches also celebrate other minor festivals linked with various saints and important beliefs. Both Churches, for instance, remember the Assumption of the Virgin Mary into heaven on August 15th.

Protestants tend to place less importance on the value of such celebrations. Whilst the Anglican Church commemorates the major festivals. Nonconformist Churches celebrate little beyond Christmas, Easter and Whitsun.

Three cycles

The Christian Year falls into three main cycles:

1] The Christmas cycle The Christian year begins with Advent which commences on the last Sunday in November. There are four Sundays in Advent and the season culminates with Christmas Day on December 25th. This is the day on which Christians throughout the world celebrate the birth of Jesus in Bethlehem. Some churches also celebrate Epiphany, on January 6th, remembering the time when the Wise Men came to visit Jesus.

2] The Easter cycle Although the Christmas cycle is the most popular festival the most important for Christians is the Easter cycle. This cycle celebrates each of the events that led up to the crucifixion and resurrection of Jesus. The cycle begins six weeks after Epiphany with the beginning of the season of Lent, traditionally a time of fasting. The day before Lent begins, Shrove Tuesday, is traditionally the time when Christians were 'shriven' by confessing their sins to a priest and then absolved from any responsibility for them

1 Do some research to discover how the date of Easter is fixed each year. What other dates are affected by the date of Easter?

2 a. What is the Christian Year?
 b. Into how many cycles is the Christian Year divided and what are they?
c. Which two Christian festivals are the most important?
d. Which two Churches place the greatest importance on the celebration of the Christian Year?

3 Write short notes on each of the following:
a. The Christmas cycle.
b. The Easter cycle.
c. The Whitsun cycle.

4 a. Explain why you think that the Christian calendar is important for many Christians.
b. Explain how you think the Christian year might affect someone living in this country who is not a Christian.

before God. On Ash Wednesday they are marked by the sign of the cross in ash on their forehead as a token of their repentance. This is the beginning of a time of self-examination and repentance leading up to the holiest Christian festival of all – Easter. Lent lasts for forty days – the length of time that Jesus spent in the wilderness being tempted by the Devil. The fast of Lent does not include any Sundays.

Easter itself is a 'moveable' feast. This simply means that, unlike Christmas, the date of Easter is not fixed. It varies from year to year. In the early Church converts to Christianity were prepared during Lent and presented for baptism on Easter Sunday. The same tradition was also linked to

Advent ~ Ascension ~ Ash Wednesday ~ Baptism ~ Christmas ~ Easter Day~ Epiphany ~ Good Friday ~ Lent ~ Nonconformist Church ~ Orthodox Church ~ Pentecost ~ Protestant ~ Roman Catholic Church ~ Whitsun

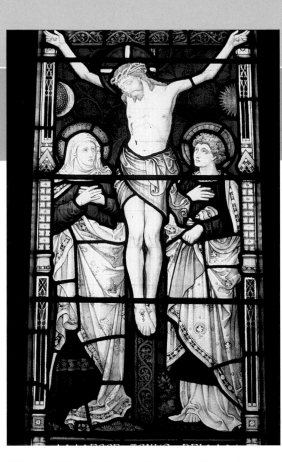

[B] Why is Good Friday the most solemn day in the Christian year?

Whitsun. Good Friday is the most solemn day in the Christian calendar. On this day Christians remember the death of Jesus on the cross. Some Christians spend a long time in church on this day meditating on this, the central belief of the Christian faith. Easter Day follows two days later. By this time the mood of Christian worship has changed from solemnity to one of hopeful anticipation. Christians meet together from midnight onwards to celebrate the resurrection of Jesus from the dead. With Easter Day the 'Easter Cycle' is complete.

3] The Whitsun cycle The third cycle of the Christian year is less important than the other two although it does include the important Whitsun festival. Before this, however, many churches celebrate Ascension Day, which comes forty days after Easter. Ascension Day remains one of the Roman Catholic 'Days of Obligation' [chief Feast Days]. Whitsun, also known as Pentecost, recalls the giving of the Holy Spirit to the first Christians on the Jewish festival of Pentecost. This day saw the birth of the Christian Church and, for some, it is an opportunity to renew their commitment to sharing the Christian message with those who do not believe. This was the original motivation behind the 'Whit Walks' which used to be such a feature of Nonconformist church life in the north of England.

8:2 From Advent to Epiphany

KEY QUESTION

WHY ARE THE
FESTIVALS OF
ADVENT,
CHRISTMAS AND
EPIPHANY
IMPORTANT IN
THE CHRISTIAN
CALENDAR?

BOX 1

JOHN 1.1-3,14

*In the beginning
was the Word and
the Word was with
God and the Word
was God. He was
with God in the
beginning. Through
him all things were
made; without him
nothing was made
that was made...
The Word became
flesh and made
his dwelling among
us. We have seen
his glory, the glory
of the One and
Only, who came
from the Father,
full of grace and
truth.*

The Christian Year starts with Advent before moving through the Christmas festival to Epiphany. Each of these festivals is closely linked to the others.

Advent

Advent ['approach' or 'coming'] is the time that the Church sets aside for preparation for the coming of Jesus at Christmas. Advent begins on the fourth Sunday before Christmas and is a time for Christians to think about:

1] The coming of John the Baptist to prepare the way for the coming of Jesus. John the Baptist was a messenger sent by God ahead of Jesus to prepare the people for his coming [box 2]. Readings from the Old Testament prophets speaking about this are an important part of Advent services.

2] The coming of the Messiah, Jesus. This coming was prophesied by the prophets in the Old Testament and by the Angel Gabriel when he appeared to Joseph [Matthew's Gospel] and Mary [Luke's Gospel]. Both of these readings are included in services before Christmas.

3] The 'second coming' of Jesus. Ever since Jesus left the earth after his resurrection Christians have been expecting him to return *[2.10]*.

Two important symbols underline the significance of Advent:

a. The Advent Wreath is a ring of greenery surrounded by five candles. The central candle is white, the symbol of purity, whilst the others are purple, symbolising penitence. One candle is lit on the first Sunday of Advent and the other candles are lit on the following Sundays. The white candle symbolises Jesus, the Light of the world, whilst the greenery reminds everyone of the eternal life that Jesus came to bring.

b. An Advent Candle is marked with numbers 1-24 and a part of the candle is burned each day. Again, the candle represents Christ, the Light of the world.

[A] What great mystery is suggested by this crib?

Christmas

At the festival of Christmas [Old English: Christes Masse] Christians celebrate the great mystery at the heart of their faith – the birth of God as a human being. This belief is called the 'Incarnation' and is explained in 2.3. Throughout the world Christians come together on Christmas Eve to celebrate this

BOX 2

LUKE 1.76-77

*You, my child, will be called a prophet
of the Most High God. You will go ahead
of the Lord, to prepare a road for him,
to tell his people that they will be saved by
having their sins forgiven.*

1 Describe TWO things that Christians prepare themselves for during Advent.

2 Why is Christmas an important festival for Christians?

3 What is the link between Christmas and Epiphany?

4 Give an account of the beliefs on which Christmas is based.

5 What do Christians celebrate on Christmas Day and how do they do it?

event in Midnight Mass. Churches are lavishly decorated for this service which, in many places, is the best attended of the year. The service may start earlier than midnight but communion will not be celebrated until Christmas Day has begun. There are also services on Christmas Day itself for the whole family when carols [hymns about Christmas] are sung and the Bible accounts of the birth of Jesus are read.

The mystery of the Incarnation is almost impossible for Christians to understand. To help them to absorb something of its meaning Orthodox Christians use icons of the Virgin Mary and her baby in their prayers. Statues of Mary and child, prominent in Roman Catholic churches, are also visual reminders to worshippers of the miracle that Christians believe to be at the heart of the Christmas festival.

Epiphany

The feast of Epiphany ['to show forth'], comes at the end of the twelve days of Christmas, January 6th, for most Christians. Orthodox Christians,

however, retain the same date for Christmas itself since that is the date on which the Church celebrated the festival for several centuries. At Epiphany three manifestations of Jesus are remembered:

a. The showing of the baby Jesus to the shepherds and Wise Men. The Wise Men were the first Gentiles [non-Jews] to recognise that there was something special about Jesus, the Saviour of the world.

b. The showing of Jesus to be God's Son when he was baptised by John the Baptist in the River Jordan.

c. The showing of the power of Jesus when he turned water into wine at his first miracle.

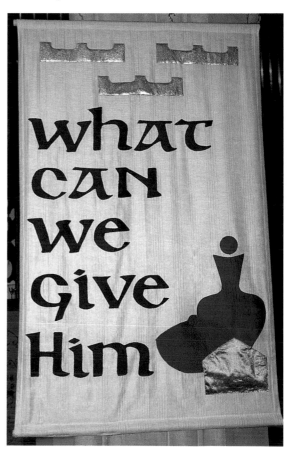

In the Glossary

Advent ~ Christmas ~ Epiphany ~ Incarnation ~ John the Baptist ~ Messiah ~ Old Testament ~ Orthodox Church ~ Roman Catholic Church ~ Sunday ~ Virgin Birth ~ Virgin Mary

BOX 3

THE APOSTLES' CREED

I believe in Jesus Christ, his only Son, our Lord. He was conceived by the power of the Holy Spirit and born of the Virgin Mary.

8:3 Lent

KEY QUESTION

WHAT IS THE IMPORTANCE OF LENT IN THE CHRISTIAN YEAR?

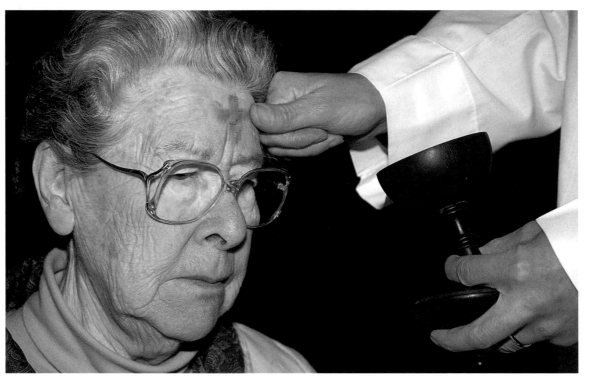

[A] Where does the ash come from for this ash cross on Ash Wednesday?

Lent is the period of forty days in the Christian year which leads up to Easter Day. The forty days are counted from Ash Wednesday through to Easter Sunday but not including Sundays. The length of Lent represents the forty days that Jesus spent fasting in the desert before his temptations at the hand of Satan [see box 1]. In the Orthodox Church the beginning of Lent is preceded by four weeks of fasting ['the Great Fast']. In the Roman Catholic Church the obligation to fast has been limited to the first day of Lent and Good Friday since 1966. Holy Week *[see 8.4]* brings Lent to a close running through from Palm Sunday to Easter Saturday.

Lent

Matthew tells us in his Gospel *[4.1]* that Jesus had just been baptised by John when 'the Spirit led him into the desert to be tempted by the Devil'. After fasting for forty days Jesus was tempted by the Devil to turn the stones around him into bread; to worship the Devil in exchange for being

(Az) **In the Glossary**

Anglican Church ~ Ash Wednesday ~ Easter Day ~ Good Friday ~ Jerusalem ~ Lent ~ Nonconformist Church ~ Old Testament ~ Orthodox Church ~ Palm Sunday ~ Roman Catholic Church ~ Satan ~ Sunday

1 How would you explain the meaning and importance of Shrove Tuesday and Ash Wednesday to Christians today?

2 a. What is Lent? b. Why do many Christians see Lent as a very important time of preparation for the time of Easter? c. What is the link between the temptations of Jesus in the wilderness and the season of Lent?

3 Read Matthew 4.1-11. Give an account of the temptations of Jesus.

4 Describe two ways in which Christians keep Lent and the reasons for them.

5 What is the link between Lent and Easter?

given all the kingdoms of the world to rule over and to jump from the pinnacle of the Temple in Jerusalem knowing that God would keep him from all harm. Each time Jesus resisted the Devil's testings by quoting words from the Jewish Scriptures. Finally the Devil left him alone for a while but the Church remembers this important time in the life of Jesus each time that it celebrates Lent.

Shrove Tuesday and Ash Wednesday are important:

1] Shrove Tuesday, the day before Lent begins. In the past Christians used up all the fat in their homes before Lent began. The fat was often used to make pancakes, so providing the people with a last chance to enjoy a feast before the fasting of Lent began. They also sought God's forgiveness and absolution from the priest before the fasting began - they were 'shriven'. Shrove Tuesday still remains in the Christian calendar although its religious significance has long since disappeared.

2] Ash Wednesday On Ash Wednesday, the first day of Lent, a special Communion Service is held in most Catholic, Orthodox and Anglican churches - Nonconformists do not keep the day. At this Communion Service an ash cross is marked on the forehead of each worshipper [A] to remind them of two things:

a. The cycle of days on which they are just beginning will lead them all the way through to the death of Jesus on the cross.

b. Lent is a time of repentance. In the Old Testament people used to wear sackcloth and ashes when they were repenting of their sins or

mourning the death of a loved one. The ash used on Ash Wednesday is obtained by burning the palm crosses given to members of the congregation at the previous Palm Sunday service. As the priest makes the mark of the cross on the forehead so he tells each worshipper: 'Remember' O man 'that dust thou art and to dust thou shalt return.' *[see box 2]*.

Anticipating the events of Good Friday, Christians are mourning the death of Jesus as well as expressing great sorrow for their own sins. Few Christians now fast seriously although some do try to carry out some continuing act of self-denial during Lent. In most churches, though, the emphasis is now placed positively upon the opportunity for spiritual renewal that Lent provides. Often special talks, Bible-studies and times of prayer are arranged for this season. This puts people in the right frame of mind to remember, and celebrate, the most important events in their faith on Good Friday and Easter Sunday.

Choose ONE out of the Roman Catholic, Orthodox or Anglican Churches. Ask a representative from one of these Churches to come into school to tell you how their own particular Church celebrates Lent and Easter. Make notes of the information that you are given in your folders.

Read Luke 19.28-44; John 13.1-17

8:4 Holy Week

Holy Week is the last week in Lent and it commemorates events in the last few days in the life of Jesus before he was crucified. In this unit we look at two of those events and the ways in which they are celebrated today.

1] Palm Sunday In the time of Jesus, Jews travelled from all over the Roman Empire to be in Jerusalem to celebrate the festival of Passover each year. They were remembering the time, hundreds of years earlier, when God had delivered the Jews from slavery in Egypt. This event, known as the Exodus, was the most important in Jewish history. It was only natural that Jesus, as a Jew, would want to celebrate this festival in Jerusalem with his disciples, it was a 'family' celebration. On the outskirts of the city Jesus sent two of his disciples to find a donkey that was tethered in a nearby village. They brought the animal back to Jesus and he sat on its back. Jesus was about to fulfil the words of the Old Testament prophet, Zechariah [box 1]. The people, and the disciples, realising that something special was happening, spread their cloaks and palm branches on the road in front of him. The crowd shouted out as Jesus rode into the city [box 2]. The welcome that they gave to Jesus showed that they recognised him to be the Messiah.

On Palm Sunday many Anglican and Catholic churches hold a special procession through the streets to re-enact this scene [A]. The procession is often led by a donkey, sometimes carrying a small child. The people follow behind waving palm crosses that they have been given in church and singing appropriate hymns. Jesus knew that he was riding towards his death and the palm crosses are a reminder to everyone of this.

2] Maundy Thursday Taken from the Latin word 'mandatum' which means 'order', Maundy

---

BOX 2

JOHN 13.14-17

Now that I, your Lord and Teacher, have washed your feet, you should also wash one another's feet. I have set you an example that you should do as I have done for you. I tell you the truth, no servant is greater than his master, nor is a messenger greater than the one who sent him. Now that you know these things, you will be blessed if you do them.

BOX 1

ZECHARIAH 9.9

Daughter of Zion [Jerusalem], rejoice with all your heart; Shout in triumph, daughter of Jerusalem! See, your king is coming to you, his cause won, his victory gained, humble and mounted on a donkey, on a colt, the foal of a donkey.

[A] Why did Jewish people gather in Jerusalem for the Passover festival?

[B] What was Jesus teaching his disciples when he washed their feet?

Thursday reminds us of the new commandment which Jesus gave to his disciples [see box 3]. Two events which happened on the first Maundy Thursday have left their mark on Christian worship ever since:

a. Jesus washed the feet of his disciples [B]. This was normally the responsibility of the most menial servant in the household. By washing the feet of his disciples, therefore, Jesus was teaching them a very important lesson about the kingdom of God. All disciples of Jesus must put themselves firmly at the service of others. In some churches the priest or minister acts out this parable in front of members of the congregation when he or she washes their feet. In the Roman Catholic Church priests celebrate Mass with their bishop who consecrates the oil that is going to be used in some of the sacraments in the coming year.

b. Jesus ate his last meal with his disciples. Known as the Last Supper, Jesus took bread at this meal, broke and blessed it and then gave some to each of his disciples with the words, 'This is my body.' Later he took a goblet of wine, blessed it and gave to his disciples saying 'This is my blood.' Christians remember this meal each time they celebrate the Eucharist. Celebrating this sacrament on Maundy Thursday is one of the most important celebrations of Holy Week.

During the Maundy Thursday Eucharist the priest wears white vestments. The Gloria is sung for the first time since Ash Wednesday and the church bells are rung for the last time before falling silent until Easter [Holy] Saturday. In some churches there follows a Watch by the cross when people pray silently as if they are watching with Jesus. Sometimes the Watch lasts until the start of the Good Friday service with members of the congregation taking it in turns to pray – so that the Watch is never broken.

▶ Work to do

1 a. Explain what happened on the first Palm Sunday.
b. Describe how many churches celebrate Palm Sunday today.
c. Explain the meaning of this day for Christians.

2 a. How was Jesus making an important statement about his life and ministry when he entered Jerusalem on a donkey?
b. Throughout his ministry Jesus saw himself fulfilling prophecies from the Jewish Scriptures. How did he do this on the first Palm Sunday?

3 Why is Maundy Thursday a particularly important day in the Christian calendar?

(A-z) In the Glossary

Anglican Church ~ Ash Wednesday ~ Bishop ~ Disciple ~ Eucharist ~ Exodus ~ Holy Week ~ Jerusalem ~ Last Supper ~ Lent ~ Mass ~ Maundy Thursday ~ Messiah ~ Old Testament ~ Palm Sunday ~ Passover ~ Priest ~ Roman Catholic Church

BOX 3

JOHN 13.34, 35

A new command I give you: Love one another. As I have loved you, so you must love one another. By this all men will know that you are my disciples, if you love one another.

8:5 Good Friday

KEY QUESTION

WHY IS GOOD
FRIDAY SUCH
AN IMPORTANT
DAY IN THE
CHRISTIAN
YEAR AND
HOW IS IT
CELEBRATED BY
THE DIFFERENT
CHURCHES?

Good Friday is the most important day in Holy Week. It is the day on which Christians look back to the crucifixion of Jesus two thousand years ago in Jerusalem. The sombre and dark mood of the day is reflected in the decor of many churches as all pictures, statues and wall-hangings are either removed or covered by a cloth. There are no flowers in the church building and the Eucharist is not celebrated between Maundy Thursday and Easter Day. All of this reminds worshippers that Good Friday is a day set aside for serious meditation upon the event which is at the very heart of the Christian faith.

Church services

Often the shared grief of Christians on this day draws them together across any denominational divide to take part in a combined act of public witness to their Christian faith. This usually takes the form of a procession led by someone carrying

[A] What does the 'veneration of the cross' involve?

a large wooden cross, just as Jesus did up the Via Dolorosa [the Way of Sorrows] in Jerusalem to Calvary. The procession visits the different churches in the area to collect more people. When they reach a central point an open-air service is held in which members of the public are invited to join.

In addition to this, most Christians try to spend some time in church on Good Friday worshipping and meditating on the death of Jesus. Different denominations, though, have their own particular ways of spending the day:

1] In Roman Catholic and some Anglican churches there is a special service which runs from noon to three o'clock in the afternoon, the last hours in the life of Jesus. The accounts of the crucifixion from all the Gospels are read since each of them brings a different perspective to what happened. A wooden cross is then laid in front of the congregation [A] and each person comes forward to kiss it [called the 'veneration of the cross']. The priest says: 'This is the wood of the cross on which the Saviour of the world died.' Prayers are said which express the deep thankfulness of the people to Jesus for sacrificing himself on the cross.

BOX 1

MARK 15.22-27

They took Jesus to a place called Golgotha, which means 'The Place of the Skull'. There they tried to give him wine mixed with a drug called myrrh but Jesus would not drink it. Then they crucified him and divided his clothes amongst themselves, throwing dice to see who would get which piece of clothing. It was nine o'clock in the morning when they crucified him. The notice of the accusation against him said: 'The King of the Jews'. They also crucified two bandits with Jesus, one on his right and the other on his left.

1 What events in the life of Jesus are specially remembered by Christians on Good Friday?

2 The day on which Jesus died is called 'Good Friday' by Christians. In what way do you think this day could be called 'good' by Christians?

3 a. Why is Good Friday so important to Christians?
b. Describe ONE way in which church worship might be different on that day compared to other days.

4 Describe how Good Friday is celebrated by either Roman Catholics or Orthodox Christians.

All Roman Catholic churches have fourteen Stations of the Cross around the outside wall of the building which illustrate, through sculpture or paintings, the different places where Jesus is thought to have stopped on his way to the cross. These Stations were originally placed in churches in the Middle Ages when it became too dangerous for pilgrims to visit Jerusalem in the Holy Land to follow in the footsteps of Jesus for themselves. Now, visiting the Stations in church is a kind of 'pilgrimage' as Christians try to share the pain and suffering of those hours. Each person slowly visits each of the Stations, kneels and says a prayer before moving on to the next [B].

2] In Orthodox Churches Good Friday is known as 'Great Friday'. The special Orthodox Good Friday liturgy is held in the evening and concentrates on the burial of Jesus. The priest carries an icon of the dead Christ, wrapped in its burial clothes, and lowers it into a stand in the middle of the church. The people gather round it holding candles as if they were at a funeral. They come forward and kiss the icon to express their love for Jesus. Later, the icon is carried around the outside of the church in a 'funeral procession,' as the church bells toll.

3] Nonconformist Churches do not have any special ritual attached to Good Friday but they do have a special service in which readings from the Gospels feature prominently. God is thanked for sending Jesus to die to save the people from their sins.

In its own way, though, this is what each church is doing on Good Friday. By going willingly to the cross Jesus openly displayed the love of God for the whole human race [box 2]. The Christian message is that it is now up to each person to respond to that love for themselves.

[B] Why do many Christians visit, and pray in front of, the Stations of the Cross on Good Friday?

BOX 2

JULIAN OF NORWICH [1342-1420]

Wouldst thou learn thy Lord's meaning in this thing? Learn it well; love was his meaning.

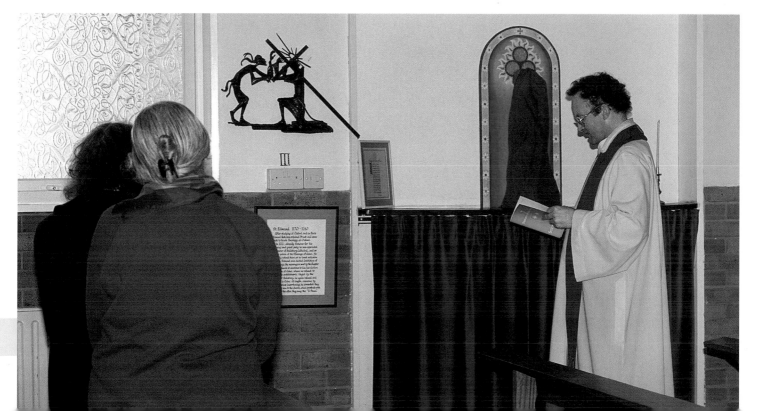

8:6 | Easter Day

WHY IS EASTER DAY SUCH AN IMPORTANT TIME FOR ALL CHRISTIANS?

The crucifixion of Jesus is celebrated by Christians, as we saw in 8.5, on Good Friday and his resurrection from the dead on Easter Day.

The Easter liturgies

The special Easter liturgies play a very important part in the celebrations of the resurrection of Jesus from the dead in Orthodox, Catholic and many Anglican churches. All of them make great use of the central symbol of Jesus, the Light of the world, overcoming the darkness of death and despair by his resurrection. This expresses why Christians believe this event to be so important.

1] The Orthodox liturgy Just as the women came to the darkened tomb on the first Easter morning so worshippers now gather outside the church before midnight. Everyone lights the candle they are carrying from the candle that the priest is holding before a procession makes its way around the church. At midnight the priest throws open the door of the church and everyone enters with their candles. The priest shouts out, 'Christ is

[A] Who went to the tomb on the first Easter morning and what did they find?

BOX I

MARK 16.1-6

When the Sabbath was over, Mary Magdalene, Mary the mother of James, and Salome brought spices so that they might go to anoint Jesus' body. Very early on the first day of the week, just after sunrise, they were on their way to the tomb and they asked each other,'Who will roll the stone away from the entrance of the tomb?' But when they looked up they saw that the stone, which was very large, had been rolled away. As they entered the tomb, they saw a young man dressed in a white robe on the right hand side and they were alarmed. 'Don't be alarmed,'he said. 'You are looking for Jesus the Nazarene, who was crucified. He has risen! He is not here.

risen,' and the people reply, 'He is risen indeed.' They all enter the church to celebrate the liturgy for resurrection day.

This liturgy is full of joy, light and expectation. The Bible readings from the Old Testament spell out the great acts of God on behalf of his people. The New Testament readings concentrate on the resurrection of Christ from the dead. The liturgy then moves towards its climax as the people receive the body [bread] and blood [wine] of Jesus in the Eucharist.' This is the most important Eucharistic celebration of the year.

2] The Catholic and Anglican liturgies The liturgy for Easter Day in these Churches can be celebrated on the Saturday evening, at midnight or on Easter morning. Often, though, it is celebrated at midnight so that the full impact of the symbolism of light and darkness which lies at the heart of the liturgy can be experienced. The Paschal candle which is carried into the church by the priest is special, having on it:

a. The Greek letters alpha and omega [the first and last letters of the alphabet]. These letters are often used to indicate the 'beginning and the

Talk it over

Why do you think that Easter is the most important festival in the Christian year?

end'.

b. A cross

c. Five small brass knobs – to show the five wounds that Jesus received on the cross [both feet, both wrists and the spear wound in his side].

This candle symbolises the risen Christ. It is lit for all services in church until Ascension Day or Pentecost. It is also lit for all baptism and funeral services in church. As the Paschal candle is carried through the darkened church so each person lights their own candle from it. The passing of the light from one person to another symbolises the good news of the Christian Gospel being passed from one person to another. Whenever the light of Christ comes into any dark situation it brings its own light. As the liturgy continues so each person is invited to renew their baptismal vows. In the early centuries of the Christian faith baptisms always took place at Easter and so this is the appropriate time for baptismal vows to be renewed. In Roman Catholic churches a baby is often baptised on Easter Day as a sign of the new life that resurrection brings.

3] Nonconformist churches In Nonconformist churches people are often up early on Easter morning to celebrate the resurrection of Jesus. It was early morning when the three women visited the tomb of Jesus to anoint his body and found it empty. The sight of the sun rising over the horizon is a reminder of light replacing darkness and of the

new life that Christ rose to bring. The same message is conveyed by the Easter eggs which are such a feature of the festival.

You can find out more about the significance of the resurrection of Jesus and its importance for Christians today in unit 2.4.

Work to do

1 a. What do Christians celebrate at Easter?
b. Why is Easter such an important time for them?

2 Describe TWO features that you might find in an Anglican or Roman Catholic service on Easter Day.

3 How do Orthodox and Catholic Christians use the symbols of light and darkness to help them express the real meaning of Easter.

[B] Why does light as a symbol play such an important part in the Easter liturgies?

In the Glossary

Anglican Church ~ Ascension ~ Baptism ~ Bible ~ Easter Day ~ Eucharist ~ Good Friday ~ Liturgy ~ New Testament ~ Nonconformist Church ~ Old Testament ~ Orthodox Church ~ Paschal Candle ~ Pentecost ~ Priest ~ Roman Catholic Church

8:7 Ascension Day and Pentecost

Easter brings to a close the two main 'cycles' of the Christian year. There are still, though, some festivals to come in the third 'cycle' and these centre around Pentecost [Whitsun] which celebrates the giving of the Holy Spirit to the disciples of Jesus on the Day of Pentecost. This event marked the birth of the Christian Church. Before that, however, comes Ascension Day, forty days after Easter Day.

Ascension Day

For Christians Ascension Day, which always falls on a Thursday, completes the sequence of events that were celebrated at Easter. The day recalls the final ascension of Christ into heaven after he had been raised from the dead and recommissioned his disciples *[see Matthew 28.16-20]*. The event marked the end of the various appearances of Jesus to groups of disciples and followers which are

---

BOX 1

ACTS 1.9-11

After he said this, he was taken up before their very eyes, and a cloud hid him from their sight. They were looking intently up into the sky as he was going, when suddenly two men dressed in white stood beside them. 'Men of Galilee,' they said, 'why do you stand here looking into the sky? This same Jesus, who has been taken from you into heaven, will come back in the same way you have seen him go into heaven.'

[A] What is the link between Ascension Day and the festival of Pentecost?

Why do you think that many Christians see a direct link between celebrating Pentecost and the work of evangelising?

1 How does Luke explain what happened to the followers of Jesus on the Day of Pentecost?

2 What do Christians celebrate at Pentecost?

3 Explain why Pentecost is an important Christian festival.

4 What was the Ascension of Jesus and how do Christians celebrate the event today?

5 Write short notes on each of the following:
a. The festival of Pentecost.
b. Ascension Day.

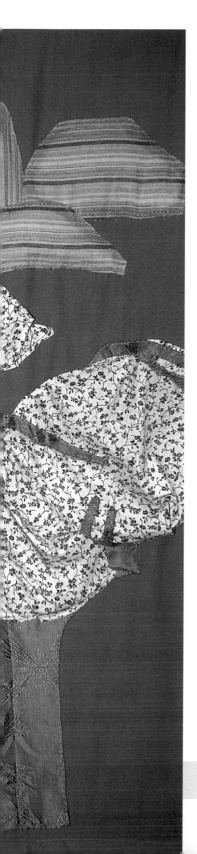

recorded in the Gospels and in the letters of Paul. You can read Luke's description of the ascension of Jesus in box 1.

The Ascension was important because it marked:

1] The final act in the earthly life of Jesus.

2] The beginning of the lead-up to the giving of the Holy Spirit to the first Christians.

3] The promise that Jesus would return to the earth at some future time to set up God's kingdom. [see box 1]. This event is known to Christians as the Second Coming.

As you will notice from Luke's description Jesus was 'seen' to ascend upwards into heaven which was located above the clouds. This description would not have caused any problems to early Christian readers who were used to locating heaven above the clouds but it makes Christians feel rather uncomfortable today. This probably explains the reluctance of most churches to celebrate the day. In the Catholic Church, however, it is one of the 'days of obligation' when worshippers are expected to attend Mass in church.

Pentecost

Fifty days after Easter the Church celebrates the giving of the Holy Spirit to the apostles on the Day of Pentecost [see 1.2]. This led to a dramatic

---

BOX 2

JOHN 14.16-26

And I will ask the Father, and he will give you another Counsellor to be with you forever - the Spirit of truth. The world cannot accept him, because it neither sees him nor knows him. But you know him, for he lives with you and will be in you. I will not leave you as orphans; I will come to you... All this I have spoken while still with you. But the Counsellor, the Holy Spirit, whom the Father will send in my name, will teach you all things and will remind you of everything I have said to you.

---

increase in the number of Christians throughout the Roman Empire. The Charismatic Movement is a recognition that the Holy Spirit is very important in the lives of Christians today [see 4.6]. This festival carries two names:

1] Whitsun [White Sunday] Traditionally new converts to Christianity were baptised at either Easter or Whitsun. For this service they wore white clothes to symbolise their new-found purity as believers in Christ. Their sins had been forgiven. In some churches this custom is maintained today with people being confirmed on this day. During confirmation the bishop, who normally takes this service, places his hands on the head of each candidate so that they might receive the Holy Spirit. This is the gift of which Jesus spoke - see box 2.

2] Pentecost [50 days] Pentecost was the name of the old Jewish harvest festival [the Festival of Weeks] which fell fifty days after the important festival of Passover at which the deliverance of the Jewish slaves from Egypt was commemorated. It was during the celebration of this festival that the first disciples received the Holy Spirit.

In the Glossary

Apostle ~ Ascension ~ Baptism ~ Bible ~ Bishop ~ Confirmation ~ Disciple ~ Easter Day ~ Holy Spirit ~ Paul ~ Pentecost ~ Roman Catholic Church ~ Whitsun

8:8 Sunday

KEY QUESTION

WHY IS SUNDAY
A SPECIAL
DAY FOR
CHRISTIANS
AND HOW
DO THEY
CELEBRATE IT?

Sunday is different from all of the other festivals covered in this unit. Each of the others is celebrated once a year but Sunday is celebrated each week. On this day, the first of the week, Christians celebrate the most important event in the Christian faith - the resurrection of Jesus from the dead.

The Sabbath Day

The custom of celebrating the Sabbath Day, the seventh day of the week, goes all the way back to the earliest times of the Jewish people. They were reminded of this in their Ten Commandments: 'Remember the Sabbath day to keep it holy.' [Exodus 20.8]. For Jews everywhere the Sabbath Day was to be a day of holiness, set apart, a day of rest, a day unlike any other in the week. It was linked with two very important events in Jewish history:

1] The day of rest that followed the six days on which God created the world [Exodus 20.11]. This link bestowed divine authority on the day. If God needed to rest after working then human beings certainly did.

2] The deliverance of the Jews from Egyptian slavery [Deuteronomy 5.15] - the event that was celebrated each year in the great Jewish festival of Passover.

As the first Christians were nearly all Jews it was natural for them to continue to observe the Sabbath Day. It was only when they were prevented from preaching and worshipping in the Jewish synagogues on this day that they began to meet together to 'break bread' on Sunday i.e. the day on which Jesus rose from the dead.

BOX 1

ST JUSTIN, 2ND CENTURY CHURCH LEADER

We all gather on the day of the sun, for it is the first day when God, separating matter from darkness, made the world; and on this same day Jesus Christ our Saviour rose from the dead.

Sunday, the Lord's Day

Jesus 'rose from the dead on the first day of the week' [Matthew 28.1] - the day after the Jewish Sabbath. By the end of the 1st century Christians had adopted this day, the 'Lord's Day', as the most appropriate time for their worship. The name 'Sunday', though, was much older than Christianity being linked in the Roman Empire with the worship of Mithras, the sun-god. As box 1 makes clear the Church did not feel uneasy adopting a day dedicated to the worship of a pagan god for their worship of God.

The Catechism of the Catholic Church, published in 1994, gives two reasons why all Catholics should make every attempt to attend church on this day:

1] Sunday is the day on which the Mass is celebrated. This celebration is at the heart of the Church's, and each individual Catholic's, spiritual

BOX 2

CATECHISM OF THE CATHOLIC CHURCH

Participation in the communal celebration of the Sunday Eucharist is a testimony of belonging and of being faithful to Christ and his Church. The faithful give witness by this to their communion in faith and charity. Together they testify to God's holiness and their hope of salvation. They strengthen one another under the guidance of the Holy Spirit…Sunday is a time for reflection, silence, cultivation of the mind and meditation which furthers the growth of the Christian interior life.

1 a. What is the Sabbath Day?
b. Why was it natural for the early Christians to set aside the Sabbath Day as their time for worshipping God?
c. Why did this arrangement eventually end?
d. Why did Christians adopt Sunday as their holy day?

2 a. Which two reasons did the Catechism of the Catholic Church put forward for Catholics making every attempt to be in church on Sunday?
b. What exception was made to this rule?

By making Sunday like every other day of the week do you think that this country has benefitted or lost out?

life. This makes Sunday '…the foremost holy day of obligation in the universal Church."
2] Sunday is the day of rest from normal work. Sunday is a day for re-creation. As such it is a day that should benefit every Christian's family, religious, social and personal life. As the Catechism puts it: 'Sunday is a time for reflection, silence, cultivation of the mind and meditation which furthers the growth of the Christian interior life' [see box 2]. Many Catholic services [the Sunday Vigil] are held on Saturday evenings and it is acceptable for Catholics to attend these if they cannot make Sunday worship.

This leniency over attending Mass on Sunday became very important when, in 1994, the law was changed in Britain to allow Sunday to be much like any other day of the week. Shops were allowed to open on Sundays although most of them were restricted to opening for a maximum of six hours on this day. This change was a surprisingly controversial move for Parliament to make. The move was opposed by trade unions representing shop workers and a group dedicated to keeping Sunday as a day different from the others in the week [Keep Sunday Special Campaign]. A further bill made it possible for horse-racing to be held on Sundays by removing the restrictions on betting on this day.

[A] Why do you think that the laws about trade on Sunday were changed in 1994?

In the Glossary

Mass ~ Passover ~ Sabbath Day ~ Sunday ~ Ten Commandments

A

ABSOLUTION The forgiveness of a person and the release of them from their guilt for sins committed.

ACTS OF THE APOSTLES The fifth book in the New Testament, tells the story of the early Church from the ascension of Jesus to Paul's imprisonment in Rome.

ADVENT The four weeks before Christmas, commemorating the first and second coming of Jesus.

ALTAR The stone or wooden table in front of the east wall of many churches, the place at which Holy Communion is celebrated.

ALTERNATIVE SERVICE BOOK The Prayer Book introduced in 1980 for Church of England worship.

ANGLICAN CHURCH The name given to a large group of Churches from all over the world who accept the leadership of the Church of England.

ANGLO-CATHOLIC The group in the Church of England which follows many Roman Catholic practices in worship, also called High Church.

ANOINTING THE SICK One of the seven sacraments practiced by the Roman Catholic Church, uses consecrated oil, formerly called 'Extreme Unction'.

APOCRYPHA The books covering the period between the end of the Old Testament and the beginning of the New Testament, only accepted by the Roman Catholic and Orthodox Churches.

APOSTLE The word apostles [meaning 'messenger'] applied to disciples when they were sent out by Jesus to preach the Gospel, title given to disciples after Day of Pentecost.

APOSTLES' CREED A Christian Creed which seems to date from the 2nd century, earliest known statement of Christian belief, used in some church services.

ARCHBISHOP The chief bishop in the Anglican and Roman Catholic Churches.

ASCENSION The ascent of Christ from earth to heaven at the end of his life, celebrated by some churches on Ascension Day.

ASH WEDNESDAY The first day of Lent, so named because of the Roman Catholic and Anglican traditions of smearing the forehead with an ash cross on this day.

ATONEMENT The Christian belief that God and humanity were brought together by the life, death and resurrection of Jesus.

B

BAPTISM Whether infant or adult the washing away of sins through sprinkling or immersion in water.

BAPTIST CHURCH The Nonconformist Church which insists that all members have been baptised as adults.

BELIEVER'S BAPTISM The practice of the Baptist Church of immersing adult believers in water to demonstrate that their sins have been forgiven.

BIBLE The holy book of Christians.

BISHOP A senior priest who presides over a diocese and has powers of ordaining and confirming.

BOOK OF COMMON PRAYER The official liturgy of the Church of England, first issued in 1549 and reissued in 1661.

BREAKING OF BREAD One of the names given to Holy Communion by Nonconformist Churches.

C

CANON 'Measuring rod', the collection of writings in the Bible which are considered to be authoritative.

CATHEDRAL The main church in a bishop's diocese.

CELIBACY A vow taken by monks, nuns and Roman Catholic priests to remain single to devote oneself to prayer and the service of God.

CHRISTMAS The festival at which Christians celebrate the birth of Jesus on December 25th.

CHRISMATION The service of confirmation in the Orthodox Church which follows directly after infant baptism, baby is anointed with chrism.

CHURCH OF ENGLAND The Church in England which severed its relations with Rome under King Henry VIII and became the Established Church under Queen Elizabeth 1.

CITADEL A Salvation Army place of worship, a place of spiritual refuge.

COMMUNION OF SAINTS The Roman Catholic belief that all people, alive and dead, are joined in an unbroken fellowship

CONFIRMATION A service in which the vows of baptism are confirmed and the Holy Spirit is given to a person.

CONVENT The religious house in which nuns live.

CONTEMPLATION An advanced state of prayer beyond meditation, a place where a person is able to contemplate (look on) God.

CREED A statement of Christian belief.

CRUCIFIX A cross which bears an image of the crucified Christ, found in Roman Catholic and Orthodox churches.

D

DAY OF PENTECOST The day on which the Holy Spirit was given to the early Christians, event celebrated at Pentecost [Whitsun].

DEVIL The evil force in Christianity opposed to God.

DISCIPLE A follower of Jesus, one of the twelve close friends chosen to accompany Jesus on his travels.

DIOCESE A district in the Church of England under the control of a bishop.

E

EASTER DAY The most important Christian day, on which Christians celebrate the rising of Jesus from the dead.

EPIPHANY The day, twelve days after Christmas, when some Christians celebrate the visit of the Wise Men to the infant Jesus.

EPISCOPACY A system of church government favoured by the Anglican and Roman Catholic Churches in which the most senior leaders are bishops.

EPISTLE A letter in the New Testament sent by a disciple of Jesus to a church or to an individual believer.

EUCHARIST 'Thanksgiving', the name favoured in the Anglican Church for Holy Communion.

EVANGELICAL A Protestant grouping of Christians who believe that the Bible is the sole authority in their church and personal lives.

EXODUS The journey of the Jews out of Egyptian slavery under Moses.

EXORCISM Practice in Pentecostal Church of casting a demon out of a person.

F

FONT Stone receptacle just inside door of church that holds the water for infant baptism.

FUNDAMENTALISM The belief of a

Protestant group that every word in the Bible is true since it came directly from God himself.

G

GOOD FRIDAY The day in Holy Week when Christians remember the death of Jesus in Jerusalem.

GOSPEL The first four books in the New Testament, contains record of the words and deeds of Jesus.

H

HAIL MARY Very important Roman Catholic prayer addressed to the Virgin Mary.

HOLY COMMUNION Most important Christian service, one of remembrance of the death of Jesus, also called Eucharist, Mass, Holy Liturgy and Breaking of Bread in different Churches.

HOLY LITURGY The service of Holy Communion in Orthodox Church.

HOLY ORDERS The ranks of bishop, priest and deacons in the Anglican, Roman Catholic and Orthodox Churches.

HOLY SPIRIT The third Person in the Christian Trinity, given to the Church after Jesus left the earth, also known as Holy Ghost.

HOLY WEEK The week in the Christian Year which begins on Palm Sunday and ends on Good Friday.

I

ICON Religious painting of Jesus, the Virgin Mary or one of the saints, used as a help to prayer in the Orthodox Church.

ICONOSTASIS Screen, covered with icons, at the front of an Orthodox church.

INCARNATION The Christian belief that Jesus, the Son of God, became a human being when he was born in Bethlehem.

INFANT BAPTISM Service in Anglican and Roman Catholic churches which brings a baby into membership of the Church.

INTERCESSION Prayer which is offered on behalf of other people.

J

JERUSALEM The most important religious city in the world, the city in which Jesus died.

JESUS PRAYER Prayer repeated many times in Orthodox worship, must contain name of Jesus and be no longer than twelve words.

JOHN THE BAPTIST The cousin of Jesus, baptised in the River Jordan at the start of the ministry of Jesus.

L

LAST SUPPER The last meal that Jesus ate with his disciples before his arrest, provided pattern for service of Holy Communion.

LENT Period of forty days running up to Easter, time of spiritual preparation for the festival.

LITURGY The public worship of any church when it is in written and set form.

LORD'S PRAYER The prayer that Jesus taught to his disciples, used in almost all acts of Christian worship.

LORD'S SUPPER Name for Holy Communion used in many Nonconformist churches.

LOURDES Pilgrimage destination for thousands of Roman Catholics in France, miraculous cures are thought to have taken place there.

M

MASS The Roman Catholic service of Holy Communion.

MAUNDY THURSDAY The day on which Christians celebrate the Last Supper and the washing by Jesus of his disciples' feet.

MEDITATION A method of prayer, involves controlling the mind and body so that both are centred on God.

MESSIAH In Jewish belief the figure sent by God to deliver his people from slavery and persecution Christians believe that Jesus was that Messiah.

METHODIST CHURCH The 18th century Nonconformist. Church based on the teachings of John Wesley.

MINISTER The leader of worship in a Nonconformist church.

MISSAL The book used in the Roman Catholic Church containing the readings and prayers for the Mass.

MONASTERY The home of a male religious order.

MONK A member of a male religious order who lives in a monastery.

MOSES The great Jewish leader who delivered the Jews from slavery in Egypt, received Ten Commandments from God on Mt Sinai.

N

NEW TESTAMENT The second part of the Bible, contains the Gospels, the Epistles and other books.

NICENE CREED The statement of Christian belief associated with the Council of Nicea held in 325, used in acts of worship.

NONCONFORMIST CHURCH A Church which does not 'conform' to the teachings of the Church of England.

NUN A woman who belongs to a religious community.

NUPTIAL MASS The Mass taken at the end of a wedding service in a Roman Catholic church, only taken if both people are Catholics..

O

OLD TESTAMENT The Jewish Scriptures, the first part of the Bible.

ORDINATION The ceremony in any Church by which a lay-person becomes a priest.

ORIGINAL SIN The Christian belief that everyone is born sinful because of the sin committed by the first man and woman.

ORTHODOX CHURCH Originally the Church of the eastern region of the Roman Empire, separated from the Roman Catholic Church in 1054

P

PALM SUNDAY The day, at the start of Holy Week, when Christians celebrate the entry of Jesus into Jerusalem on a donkey.

PARABLE Story told by Jesus carrying a spiritual or a moral lesson.

PASCHAL CANDLE A tall candle lit in church services for the forty days between Easter Day and Ascension Day.

PASSOVER The Jewish festival at which the Exodus of the Jewish slaves from Egypt is celebrated

PAUL Outstanding leader of early Church, writer of many epistles in the New Testament.

PENANCE Penalty placed on person by priest during confession as a demonstration that they are truly sorry for their sins.

PENTECOST The Jewish harvest festival celebrating the giving of the Ten Commandments to Moses, also called Shavuot and the Feast of Weeks.

PENTECOSTAL CHURCH Church formed at

beginning of 20th century, worship based on the gifts of the Holy Spirit.

PETER The most dominant of Jesus' disciples, became a leader in the early Church.

POPE 'Papa', the leader of the Roman Catholic Church, believed to be the successor of Peter as Bishop of Rome

PRESBYTERIAN Nonconformist Church formed in 17th century, merged in England with Congregational Church in 1972 to form the United Reformed Church.

PRIEST An official minister of religion, ordained and so qualified to dispense the sacraments.

PROPHET A man or woman sent by God, sent pass on God's message to the people.

PROPHETS One of three sections in the Jewish Scriptures.

PROTESTANT A member of a Christian Church based on the principles of the Reformation.

PULPIT Raised platform at front of church from which a sermon is delivered.

PURGATORY Roman Catholics believe that almost everyone spends time in purgatory after death being prepared for heaven, a state between earth and heaven.

Q

QUAKERS Nonconformist Church based on the teachings of George Fox, formed in the 17th century, also known as the 'Society of Friends'.

R

RECONCILIATION The sacrament of the Roman Catholic Church which brings together God and human beings, involves confession of sins.

REFORMATION The religious revolution in the 16th century, led to the break-up of the Catholic Church and the formation of many Protestant Churches.

REQUIEM MASS The Mass said in Catholic Churches during funerals.

RESERVED SACRAMENT Consecrated bread and wine which are kept in the tabernacle and used for people who take communion in their homes.

ROMAN CATHOLIC CHURCH The community of believers throughout the world who owe their allegiance to the Pope, the successor of Peter.

ROSARY 'Rose-garden', a string of beads used by some Roman Catholics as an aid to prayer.

ROYAL DOORS The doors in the middle of the icononasis in an Orthodox church, the priest passes through the doors to take the elements of bread and wine from the High Altar to the people during Holy Liturgy.

S

SABBATH DAY The Jewish day of rest on the last day of the week.

SACRAMENT An outward and visible sign of an inward, spiritual blessing.

SACRAMENT OF RECONCILIATION The sacrament which gives absolution and forgiveness to Roman Catholics for their sins, previously known as penance.

SAINT A person well-known for the holiness of their life, the Roman Catholic Church canonises people after their death.

SALVATION ARMY A Nonconformist organisation formed in the middle of the 19th century, most well-known for its work amongst the poor.

SANCTUARY The area around the altar at the front of a church.

SATAN See Devil.

SECOND COMING The Christian belief that Jesus will return to the earth to set up God's kingdom.

SECOND VATICAN COUNCIL The Council of the Roman Catholic Church held between 1962 and 1965, made many decisions which modernised the Church.

SHROVE TUESDAY The day before Lent begins.

STATIONS OF THE CROSS Pictures or sculptures around the outside wall of a Roman Catholic church, indicate the fourteen places where Jesus is thought to have stopped on his way to crucifixion.

SUNDAY Day adopted by Christians as day for worship, first day of the week as Jesus rose on this day.

SYNOPTIC GOSPELS The three Gospels [Matthew, Mark and Luke] which have a similar approach to the life of Jesus and have much material in common.

T

TEN COMMANDMENTS The laws given to Moses by God on Mt Sinai.

THIRTY-NINE ARTICLES The statement of belief first accepted by the Church of England in 1574.

TORAH The first five books of the Jewish Scriptures, the books of the Law.

TRANSUBSTANTIATION Roman Catholic belief that the bread and wine in the Mass become the body and blood of Jesus.

TRINITY The Christian belief in one God in three Persons - the Father, the Son and the Holy Spirit.

U

UNITED REFORMED CHURCH The Church formed in England from a merger between the Congregational and Presbyterian Churches in 1974.

V

VIA DOLOROSA 'The Way of Sorrows', the pathway in Jerusalem which Christ is thought to have taken on his way to execution.

VIATICUM 'Food for the journey', the taking of Holy Communion before a person is expected to die.

VIRGIN BIRTH The belief of many Christians that Jesus was miraculously conceived in the womb of Mary by the Holy Spirit.

VIRGIN MARY Mary, the mother of Jesus, the subject of great devotion by Roman Catholics.

VOTIVE CANDLE A candle lit in a Catholic church to accompany a prayer.

W

WALSINGHAM Christian pilgrimage destination in Norfolk, England.

WHITSUN 'White Sunday', also known as Pentecost, the festival at which Christians thank God for the gift of the Holy Spirit.

WORLD COUNCIL OF CHURCHES The umbrella organisation which brings together most of the world's Churches.

WRITINGS A division of the Jewish Scriptures along with the Torah and the Prophets.